Part-Time Nomads

Part-Time Nomads
Traveling the World by Bicycle
Copyright © 2023 by Anne M. Breedlove

All rights reserved. No part of this book may be reproduced or transmitted in any form or by any means without written permission from the publisher and author.

Additional copies may be ordered from the publisher for educational, business, promotional or premium use.
For information, contact ALIVE Book Publishing at: alivebookpublishing.com, or call (925) 837-7303.

Book and cover design by Alex P. Johnson

ISBN 13
978-1-63132-203-7

Library of Congress Control Number: 2023910491

Library of Congress Cataloging-in-Publication Data
is available upon request.

First Edition

Published in the United States of America by ALIVE Book Publishing and ALIVE Publishing Group, imprints of Advanced Publishing LLC
3200 A Danville Blvd., Suite 204, Alamo, California 94507
alivebookpublishing.com

PRINTED IN THE UNITED STATES OF AMERICA

10 9 8 7 6 5 4 3 2 1

Part-Time Nomads

Traveling the World by Bicycle

Anne M. Breedlove

Alive Book Publishing

*The bike will transform anyone
who is willing to let it happen.*

Ina-Yoko Teutenberg

To Jim

*We couldn't have done it
without each other.*

CONTENTS

1. Anne & Jim Discover Cycle Touring / Dordogne, France / 1997 — 2
2. We Get Our Feet Wet / Sacramento Valley / 1999 — 14
3. Jim Buys a Tent / Stanislaus County / 2000 — 26
4. We Go Au Naturel / Harbin Hot Springs / 2000 — 36
5. *A Seed is Planted / St. Cloud, Florida / 1960s* — 46
6. Then We Get Lost / Lost Coast / 2000 — 54
7. Lavaland / Mt. Lassen / 2000 — 66
8. If the World Hands You Lettuce Make a Salad / Santa Barbara County / 2000 — 78
9. Rock On / Death Valley / 2001 — 88
10. *Anne Gets First Ten Speed / Rensselaer County / 1970* — 104
11. Snow For Easter / Siskyou County / 2001 — 110
12. We B Animals / Yosemite / 2001 — 126
13. Volcano Land / Medicine Lake / 2002 — 138
14. We Go Radioactive / San Benito County / 2003 — 146
15. *Anne & Jim Become An Item / San Francisco / 1974* — 158
16. Blown Away / Skamania County / 2002 — 168
17. Pedaler's Paradise / South Island New Zealand / 2002 — 178
18. Following the Hot Water / Idaho / 2003 — 200
19. Snow & Ice / Arizona / 2005 — 216
20. *Jim & Anne Tie the Knot / Europe Honeymoon / 1977* — 232
21. Pub Crawl / Ireland / 2005 — 244
22. Rain and Shine / Big Island, Hawaii / 2007 — 264
23. Roly-Poly-Land / New Hampshire & Maine / 2007 — 278
24. Game Changers — 289
25. Postscript — 295
Lessons Learned On The Road — 297

FOREWORD

Cycling with Anne into the unknown has been one of the most uplifting experiences of my life. Together, we faced lonely roads, big trucks and off-the-road forest camping among the bears. We started out simple, heading for a motel and restaurant, but wound up hiding in the middle of nowhere, together. Together is the key word. On the road we depended on each other. Anne was the navigator; I was the mechanic: not an equal split. Anne had the harder part, picking roads away from traffic while I patched flat tires, greased chains, tightened screws.

Actually, cycling has little to do with bicycles for me. It has to do with being on our own, homeless in a strange place, between places, moving forward. It was otherworldly for me. Anne was, and always is, my home; wherever we were, we belonged together.

Our cycling adventures began in the back country behind our house and gradually went much farther. Eventually, we carried our home along, too—a tent, sleeping bags, and a stove. Water was a big deal, it's heavy. Getting water from a creek is necessary so I bought a water filter to be safe.

Wherever we went, people would ask the same three questions: "Where are you from?"; "Where are you going?"; "How long have you been on the road?" I nicknamed these friendly people "Mosquitoes" because we were preoccupied with figuring things out and needed time to rest.

Before long, California wasn't big enough for us, so we ventured to a few other states and eventually New Zealand, and Ireland. But we always got back home okay. Home seemed strange at first; after weeks away you get used to the road, and that seems normal.

The best part of cycle touring for me is being with Anne. Being together in sometimes-difficult situations, in the middle of nowhere, I was always comforted having Anne by my side. It was me and her against the world.

Anne always rode first with me behind. She thought it was that way because she was slow and I was a gentleman, but actually, it was because she was the navigator and I was just following along.

When the day was done, we'd search for a safe, hidden spot to set up our tent. Even though I was the one who usually decided where the "safe place" was, the *real* reason I felt safe was because of the person I rode with—Anne.

Anne is a smart, savvy woman with a heart of gold. I am so lucky to have found someone with such a sublime character. I will always be with her no matter where we go.

—Jim Eldredge

ACKNOWLEDGMENTS

To Katharine H. for teaching me how to flesh out a story. To Erin V.R. for providing polish and focus. And to Maureen M. for cheering me on, chapter by chapter.

INTRODUCTION

The ad in the back of Bicycling magazine read: "Self-guided bicycling tours in rural France." Eight days on furnished bikes, in pre-arranged lodging opened our eyes to the possibilities of bicycle travel.

PART-TIME NOMADS tells how we metamorphosed from middle-aged, suburban working parents to international bicycle travelers. For ten years we stole time from work and parenting to bicycle 10,000 miles in seven states and three countries. Starting in Northern California with "credit card cycling," gradually our trips became more ambitious, and our gear got good enough so we could be fully loaded and self-contained.

Our learning curve was as steep as Yosemite's 9,943-foot Tioga Pass. We pedaled through rain and snow and car exhaust, sang at the top of our lungs to ward off bears, and soaked in clothing-optional hot springs. We struggled with our differences as a couple. I'm an extrovert and a planner. Jim is a machinery-loving introvert who likes surprises. We weren't always on the same page as we tried to stay safe and sane and married. Along the way, "Can we?" morphed into a gleeful "We can do it!"

ONE

Jim & Anne Discover Cycle Touring

For our twentieth wedding anniversary, Jim and I wanted to do something special. In the two decades since our four-month honeymoon traversing Europe by train, life got in the way: jobs, two kids, and a mortgage greatly limited our travels. We were really itching to do something adventuresome again, just the two of us. Both kids were in high school and not so fond of traveling with us anymore. Our gaze returned to Europe, specifically to France. None of the countries we visited in '77 captivated us quite the way France did. In France, we fell in love with a country and an aesthetic. We were keen to return.

We only had two weeks, so Jim said, "Paris, for sure, but I want to do something different."

"What could that be?" I wondered, knowing my husband's proclivity for spontaneity. Then, one rainy winter weekend while browsing Moe's Books on Telegraph Avenue in Berkeley, I spied a bicycling magazine. Perusing the classifieds, I found a tiny three-line ad for "self-guided" French bicycle tours. It was a mom-and-pop operation run by a Canadian couple out of Manitoba—Ruth loved all things French, her husband, Rick, was a mechanic, and they both liked to travel so they started a travel business. "Self-guided" meant they booked accommodations, provided equipment, and transported possessions; all their clients had to do was follow their maps and cycle rural France. It definitely qualified as different. We took a while to commit. How hard would it be? Were we strong enough? We spent the spring months leading up to our departure cycling as many miles as we could. Jim negotiated a 9/40 work schedule that gave him every other Friday off at his job as a chemical engineer managing the wetlands at the Richmond refinery. I was halfway through a master's degree in history, trying to keep my freelance business afloat in spite of the devastating impact the Mac computer was having on graphic artists. Every other week we could put in a full day of cycling while the kids were in school and most of the world was at work.

Jim also worried the furnished bikes wouldn't measure up to his high standards. He knew there were two kinds of clusters: small sprockets with high gears for speed, and big sprockets with low gears for comfort. Most people didn't know this, bought the standard high gears, and had a miserable time because they didn't have the muscles or stamina for speed, especially in the hilly Bay Area. He wanted us to have fun, and worried the bikes would have racing gears.

The first week of June we bid adieu to the pouting kids (they were not happy to learn they'd be sharing the house with their grandmother the first week and their aunt the second). Our time in Paris would be a bit of a homecoming: we checked into our honeymoon hotel, *Henri IV,* an extremely funky and worse than shabby chic hotel on *Ile de la Cité*—oh, how the memories came rushing back. We spent five days retracing our steps and making new memories.

Then, we boarded a train for the small market town of *Gourdon,* deep in the *Dordogne.* Ruth, a trim and fit brunette in her thirties, met us at the train station. She loaded our suitcases into her rusty Citroën, and as she navigated the squirrelly streets to our lodgings, she launched into details about the tour, the region, cycling, and markets. Distracted and going a little too fast, she raised a bit of dust turning onto the crushed stone driveway of a roomy, relatively modern home set atop an expansive yard just beyond the perimeter

Chapter 1

of the historical town limits. A rotund Madame Jeanne, in provincial a flowered dress, came down the walkway, "*Bienvenue à Gourdon.*"

"*Je suit heureuse de faire voter connaissance,*" I chirped, remembering the line from my introductory French textbook. As we made small talk, a scruffily dressed Rick arrived in a beat-up van with our Trek bikes. Jim left us and immediately began checking them out and talking shop with Rick. Ruth took the opportunity to depart, and Jeanne lead me to our room.

The next morning, we entered the dining room and found an *À Volonté* (serve yourself) breakfast of orange juice, hot coffee, tea, croissants, baguettes, butter, and little jars of jam arranged around a huge bouquet of flowers on a dark mahogany sideboard.

A young couple from Chicago, Dian and Kurt, were on the last day of their tour celebrating their graduation from law school. "Oh." they said, "It was so hard, the hills here are *so* steep." Jim and I looked at each other and wondered what we got ourselves into; they were so much younger than us.

After loading a few essentials and leaving most of our things for Rick to transport to that night's lodging, we bid adieu to Madame Jeanne and set off. Our maps were color coded; yellow lines highlighted the shortest route to that night's lodgings, red lines were additional loops for those so inclined to explore more. We followed the yellow line north and made it to the small market town of Souillac before 11 a.m. We knew from experience that French shops closed at noon, so we quickly bought what we needed for a picnic lunch: paté, cheese, a baguette, bottle of wine, fruit, and two little pastries. Just beyond the town, we followed a dirt path down to the riverbank where we found a rustic table and benches made out of rough-hewn tree trunks. We enjoyed our well-earned feast as the wide, brown *Dordogne* slowly rolled past us. Jim summed it up best on a postcard to his father: "Paris seems less interesting."

We realized we were ahead of schedule, so we took an optional loop and ended up in the sleepy village of *Peyrillac-et-Millac*. Sharp eyes, Jim noticed the door of the church was open. In we went and found the cool, quiet space of the twelfth-century Romanesque building filled with art and intriguing objects: stations of the cross, statues, paintings, chandeliers, alcoves filled with flickering votive candles, and dozens of small marble plaques carved with the word "Merci" filling one wall. Every village had a church, and though the size and era varied, we found most open during the day, free of charge, and beautiful. Ruth's guide included information on many prestigious châteaux and castles, but we much preferred the humble village churches. We could enjoy them on our own terms, just the two of us, whereas tours required one to stick to a schedule, pay a bundle, and be herded in a group. The village churches suited us just fine.

A few miles past the village, I noticed a peeling wood sign, *Moulin de la Tour,* enticing us down a tree-lined alley. As we stopped in front of a rundown stone dwelling, a middle-aged man in a blue sleeveless T-shirt and dirty, green apron came into the courtyard from behind an ancient, vast door and welcomed us in for a tour. Jean-Pierre had just started crushing a new batch of walnuts. We followed him into a dark, cold room. A vertical stone wheel, two feet in diameter, was rolling around and around a massive horizontal slab five feet in diameter that was belted with an iron lip to keep the walnut mash from spilling out. All the movement was generated from a massive iron-and-wood-gear structure dating from the sixteenth century. Jean-Pierre led us back out across the courtyard to the bottling room where he pulled out a knife, started slicing a baguette, then opened a new bottle of oil and drizzled some on the slices. Divine, we bought a bottle and Jim nestled it carefully in his pannier.

We didn't arrive at that night's farmhouse, *La Ferme Fleurie in Vitrac*, until 7 p.m. Our host, a vivacious Madame Martine, came running out, *"Zut alors!"* she exclaimed, *"Vous etes très tard. Ça va bien? Quelques problèmes?"* she asked as she led us into her cobwebbed, cavernous, ancient barn crammed with dusty and rusty old farm equipment. It took a moment for our eyes to adjust to the dim light and find a space to park the bikes as we reassured her we were fine. She was terribly worried about us. Dinner started promptly at 7:30; we needed to shower and get dressed appropriately, *"Vite, très vite!"* she exclaimed as she herded us into the farmhouse and up the stairs to our room.

We were the last ones to be seated in the family-run and farm-supplied restaurant across the courtyard. Converted from a utilitarian shed, the charming, intimate room had only six tables. The rough rock walls were softened by flickering candles and flowers on crisp, white tablecloths. We were seated in a corner that removed us from the center a bit. The soft murmurs made it clear we were the only non-French speakers in the room. All but one of the tables was like ours, with couples; the table closest to the kitchen seated a distinguished, older foursome.

Then courses began, one after another, each with wine. Eight o'clock turned into nine, then ten; we struggled to stay upright, wondering when the meal would end. We certainly were hungry enough to eat all they put in front of us, but we were plenty tired. Finally, after they served what we assumed was the final course at 11 p.m., we got up to leave. *"Mais non!"* cried the maître-d' — coming between us and the door. You must stay, there's another course, the best for last. We sank back into our chairs, embarrassed to make a scene and managed to put away the dessert course before finally being allowed to return to our rooms just before midnight. Between the day's workout and the formidable meal, we were both asleep within seconds of resting our heads on the pillows.

* * *

Two days later, as we were cycling in the pouring rain from the town of *Les Eyzies* to the new, duplicated cave paintings of *"Faux" Lascaux*, we stopped briefly under an awning in a quiet village. Jim pointed to a sign in a window across the street: *Repas Au Restaurant*. We knocked on the door and a hunched-over old lady dressed all in black welcomed us into her kitchen, with a roaring fire in an immense fireplace, a scene straight out of the nineteenth century. She sat us at a thick, rough, wooden table with creaking chairs. Without saying a word, she put down two bowls of piping hot soup, half a bâtard of dark bread, a big slab of butter, and poured two small tumblers of red wine from an unlabeled bottle. The soup warmed our damp bodies and the wine soothed our anxiety about having to cycle another twenty miles in the rain.

Our last night found us at a sheep and rabbit farm run by the widow Madame Odette. Unlike Mesdames Jeanne and Martine, who wore provincial floral house dresses, Odette welcomed us in slim, worn work pants and rubber boots. She converted the spare bedrooms in her farmhouse to a *gîte* (bed and breakfast) to help pay her bills. We were put in the attic, with a high, steep, sloped ceiling and a killer view of the countryside. The second of our two tour dinners was that night at *Le Vieille Tours*, yet another farm/lodging/restaurant combo. There was a hitch though—it was two miles away and we had to get there on our own steam. No cars or taxis were available in these boondocks. We were deep in the Lot. So we dolled ourselves up in the fanciest clothes we had, smushing out the wrinkles, and biked to the restaurant. What choice did we have? We looked around and hid the bikes in the bushes before we waltzed in, no one the wiser.

After yet another unparalleled dining experience, five courses in just under three hours, we retrieved the bikes and made our way back. It was twilight, and a strong wind swirled around us with the moon providing enough light through the passing clouds for us to make our way. Bats flitted about; we felt their presence more than saw them. Our bike route followed a ridge so we could make out the hills undulating into the distance. So entranced by the magic of the moment we dared not speak. As we neared Madame Odette's, a herd of sheep panicked at the clicking sound of our bicycles and bolted—running away from but parallel to us, a vague white floating agitated mass in a field of dark.

Needless to say, our eight days in the *Dordogne* blew us away, our love affair with France reignited. The cycling was sheer bliss, and as we pedaled the back roads from village to village, we fell in love with France all over again. We decided that somehow this trip was only just the beginning.

We could and would figure out how to travel not just France, but the world, on our own steam and with our own bicycles. Number One on our list upon our return home was how to start. While Jim re-assessed our bikes and started making an equipment list, I went to bookstores and the library, searching out nearby routes and guidebooks. Over the next few years, and in our own backyard, we explored on our own terms and at our own pace.

Chez Bastit driveway

Moulin de la Tour walnut press

Les Eyzies

Gourdon street market

Village church near Rocamadour

Madame Odette's gite

TWO

Jim & Anne Get Their Feet Wet

Upon our return from France's Dordogne, Jim said our bikes were outfitted only for day rides; to tour he wanted to swap out some components and buy panniers to carry clothes and gear, and racks to hold the panniers. He spent a lot of time at REI, various bike shops, and in the garage. It fell to me to search for suitable routes, so I scoured the library and bookstores and studied maps. Even though we were keen to dive in, it took far longer than we anticipated; I was still working on a master's degree in history, our son, Oliver, was graduating from high school and preparing for college, our daughter, Eleanor, was a very active teenager, and Jim's work continued to demand more of him than I cared for. It was almost two years before we took our first solo voyage.

Eventually, on a lovely spring morning, we drove our blue station wagon with the bikes on the roof to the Sierra Nevada town of Auburn. We chose it because it was about 100 miles south of Chico, where Oliver was finishing up his first year of college. We figured with three days up and three days back, we could get a taste of the Mother Lode and the Sacramento Valley.

As we pulled up to the police department, Jim, the introvert, insisted on staying in the car. "Someone's gotta keep guard over the bikes." He coaxed me, the extrovert, into going inside and Dealing with People. "You're better at that sort of thing."

So I walked inside and explained, "My husband and I needed to find a safe place to leave our car for six days while we ride our bikes to Chico and back. Do you have any suggestions?"

"Sure, we can help you out," said the cheerful, bursting-out-of-her-uniform woman behind the counter, directing me to a numbered parking spot inside the gated lot behind the building. As I walked out the door and without missing a beat she said, "Have fun."

For this trip, we'd be "credit card touring." We'd charge all purchases—motels, restaurants, groceries—you name it. Our bikes were tricked out in sparkling new equipment. We each carried a roomy handlebar bag and two panniers (not waterproof; we'd soon discover that was a mistake) that clipped on to racks on our back wheels, packed with a couple of street outfits, PJs, some toiletries, and not much else.

We made our way through the quaint streets of downtown Auburn, past reminders of the town's gold-rush origins, climbed over the freeway, and headed north on Highway 49. We soon discovered one of the more frustrating Lessons of long-distance cycle travel, Pick Your Poison, some times both options at a fork in the road stink but ya gotta take one of them.

Major roads are the shortest and fastest route between two places, but are a constant struggle with traffic. Back roads imply peace and quiet, but typically are poorer in quality, meander around (adding extra miles) and have a lot more uppies and downies. Not yet aware of this Catch-22, we immediately opted to escape the traffic and found ourselves on a bucolic back road that soon revealed its true colors. We flew down a steep dramatic descent, all the way to a tributary of the American River that was chock-a-block with rafters. Once we finished checking out the rafting, we had to climb back up the steep canyon. Before long, there was another descent, and then another climb. Oh, we had no idea how roly-poly Northern California's back roads really were, but our thighs told us that night. Up and down, up and down. I wondered how much time Ruth put into choosing her yellow and red routes in the Dordogne?

After slogging across the foothills rather than with them (this would be one of the hardest navigational skills for me to master—learning to pick roads that ran parallel to the terrain), we found ourselves lounging on the soft bed of a lovely B&B in Nevada City's quaint downtown. Yes, we were sore, yes we were tired, but once we were off the saddles for the day, and in such a lovely setting, well, we felt like a million bucks. Our reaction was much like Rose Sayer's after going down the rapids in *The African Queen*: "I never dreamed that any mere physical experience could be so stimulating."

We covered a measly thirty-five miles that physically felt like sixty. But now, we had the evening to relax and a bounce in our steps when we walked to dinner. What's not to love about the way the day turned out? Lesson #1, Pick Your Poison, was forgotten, temporarily.

We arose bright-eyed and bushy-tailed, eager for the breakfast part of our B&B. The goal for our second day was to get to Oroville; my guidebook led me to believe that would be the next town with lodgings. Unlike our first day, where we expected to cover thirty-five miles, today we had to cover fifty. We started with some trepidation about how many roly-polies we would face that day, and ran into Lesson #2: Elevation, Elevation, Elevation. One doesn't think too much about it in a car, just gun the engine a little more for the climbs, but it's impossible to ignore the elevation when cycling five hours through foothills. Today's fifty miles was much easier than yesterday's thirty-five because it was mostly downhill.

Oroville introduced us to Lesson #3: Where's the Food? We did the distance, settled into a twentieth-century-cheesy motel, but when we headed out to eat, we found an empty, forlorn downtown of rundown motels, shoddy restaurants, and dive bars. And no grocery stores. The *Dordogne* it was not. We were starving and had to settle for junky, greasy-spoon food.

* * *

Day three's destination was the reason for the route — the college town of Chico. After an easy day cycling along the gently rolling border between foothills and valley, we feathered our bikes around the bustling downtown and checked into the modest University Inn, popular with the parent crowd. We moseyed on over to the campus, where we found Oliver keen to give us a tour, even including the craziness of his coed dorm. The kids were nice enough, but I detected a "head's-up/parent-here" look in their eyes as we were led around and introduced, and Oliver's sigh of relief when we finally left. He took us for a long walk through the pretty campus, under the dark canopy of Big Chico Creek, around the stately, three-story pink Bidwell mansion, built in the 1860s. Returning to downtown — thank goodness Chico is fairly compact — we settled for dinner in a student hot spot, Woodstock's Pizza. A little worried about what we were doing, Oliver grilled us over hot pizza and cold beers about the ride so far. We did our best to reassure him that we knew what we were doing (ha!), and made plans to drive back up in a few weeks for the summer exodus.

The temperature was pleasantly cool next morning when we took off bright and early. The ride that day was a slick glide south/southwest through the fertile Sacramento Valley. But while it was a deliciously flat day, it was also a curiously rigid ride. The vast majority of roads in the valley were built in a grid pattern. We spent most of the day riding due south for five or ten miles, then a sharp right turn west for a mile or so, with a sharp left south for another long straight stretch south.

We pedaled through vast agricultural farmland, watched farm workers and big machinery in the fields, and occasionally, we'd see a crop duster. Jim didn't like that; he didn't want us to be anywhere near the fumes. We saw dozens of crops, many we had no idea what they were and wished there were signs to tell us—nut or fruit. Olive trees were easier to recognize with the distinctive two-tone color of their leaves. Sunflowers were a delight to pass, while rice paddies were frustrating (because of the plants' insatiable need for water in our parched state). Every field was connected to the crisscrossing network of irrigation canals that fed the crops. Our destination for day four was Colusa, fifty flat-as-a-pancake miles, but we didn't rush, so entranced were we by the verdant landscape.

When we saw how close we were to the Delevan National Wildlife Refuge, we routed further west. Here's where Jim's choice of tire, Schwalbe, came in handy. No racing enthusiast would ride with tires as thick and durable as ours, but while they made for slower pedaling, they gave us great flexibility on crummy roads. The roads through the refuge were rough dirt and off limits to automobiles, but we just skirted around the gate and made our way straight down the middle, doing our best to avoid the washboards (ridges formed on dirt roads by vehicles that travel too fast—one can get a headache bouncing incessantly over the ridges).

We had the place to ourselves. Exquisite tracts of marshland on both sides, the place was loaded with so many birds. I'm more of a flora person myself, while Jim is much better at fauna. Beyond the flocks of ducks and geese, I had no idea what we were looking at. Jim recognized some: sandpipers pecking their beaks in the mudflats, stilts—pretty in black-and-white with long, thin, pink legs, flamingo-esque. And then some tiny ones that seemed almost tropical with bright yellows, blues, and greens. There were only a few of those, but they stood out. We later learned they migrate all the way to tropical Mexico during our winter.

We stopped for a leisurely picnic lunch. Lesson #4: It Ain't Over Until It's Over. We pedaled into Colusa several hours later than we planned, it was almost 6 p.m., only to discover not only were there no rooms at the inn, there were NO inns! Zip, zilch, nada. No hotels, no motels, no campgrounds, nothing. We had covered sixty miles thanks to our avian diversion, and now we had nowhere to spend the night.

Jim was the mechanic, I was the navigator, and we were in a pickle because my plans put us in a place with nowhere to stay. My map indicated the likeliest nearest lodging was another ten miles to the west. Ouch, we had to pedal into a setting sun to get to a freeway interchange. As we approached, we could see the town of Williams on the far side of the freeway. Hilarious but true: our biggest climb that day was mounting the Highway 5 overpass—fourteen feet. We arrived past dusk to an oasis of lights and delights—motels, restaurants, fast food, gas stations—all located to serve the motorists blazing north and south on Highway 5, so ironic. We had spent four days cycling rural roads only to find ourselves surrounded by the ugly reality of California car culture. Oh, the shame; I was supposed to be the navigator and now we had to race an additional ten miles to get to a place to stay as twilight turned to dark, with no headlights to protect us. I was equal parts mortified and terrified as we made our way west.

"Look," Jim exclaimed, "It's Granzella's." (a great family-run Italian place, we knew it well from many NorCal car-camping trips with the kids). Though we never really noticed before (because we never needed it), they also had a hotel. Right away Jim pipes up: "You go in and book a room; I'll watch the bikes."

"No way—it's your turn." I insisted.

"But you're not strong enough to protect the bikes. And make sure you get a nonsmoking room, oh, and a quiet room, away from the parking lot and the freeway. And a room big enough to fit the bikes. We've gotta have the bikes in the room." Precedents were being set, patterns established on this first independent ride.

Next day we had to retrace yesterday's extra ten miles. Our goal, Marysville, was practically due east from Williams. As we climbed the overpass, we both noticed some rocky hills in the distance, much closer than the Sierras could be. The craggy horizon line got closer and larger and proved to be one of the most dramatic incongruities of the Sacramento Valley, Sutter Buttes. Remnants of a dormant volcano, a million-plus years old, the distinctive jagged profile rises more than 2,000 feet above the valley. As much fun as an outdoor movie, we had the buttes in our sights for almost two hours. It was a pretty sweet, several-hundred-feet climb through isolated ranch land.

Gee, it took me until our fifth day of cycling to realize a happy Lesson, #5: The World is a Wondrous Place. If we only take the time to really look and listen, it will reveal its magic to us. I'm a noisy, busy, pushy extrovert, and yet there I was falling in love with the magic, the Zen, the solitude of pedaling for hours each day, and quietly observing the endlessly surprising California landscape as it unfolded before us.

Clearly, California is not the Dordogne and solo cycling is certainly harder than self-guided tours. The highs were higher and the lows were lower; we realized how coddled we had been in France. We suffered some but rose to the occasion, and at the end of each day we knew we were stronger and proud that we had made it. We were stimulated; we caught the bait. Cycle touring is a unique taste, difficult (if not impossible for most people) to acquire, but once we acquired it, there was no going back. We were humbled and hooked, in spite of the myriad challenges.

Our last day, we had to cover forty-five miles, with a climb of more than 1,200 feet from the valley back to Auburn. Yet, it was easier than we expected because after five days on the road, we were in better shape than we realized. When we pulled into the police station parking lot, we didn't even bother to check in, we just loaded our bikes and gear and headed to Edelweiss Restaurant on High Street. Jim slid right into the unmetered spot in front of the restaurant, starting another pattern: he'd only eat in restaurants where he could see the bikes while dining—not an easy feat. We both got yummy omeletes, their famous homemade muffins on the side with butter and marmalade, plus hot coffee—and yet another tradition started: finding a restaurant on the way home to enjoy a great, big, celebratory meal.

"So," Jim said as he steered the station wagon onto the freeway, "next trip, let's pack a tent. And two sleeping bags.

CHAPTER 2

23

I'll do the research and get really, really lights ones. And I can carry them." *Oh no,* I thought, as we left downtown Auburn for the freeway, *a man and his toys, how are we going to be able to ride loaded down with more gear?*

Auburn Police Department parking lot

Covered bridge north of Oroville

North Table Mountain

THREE

Jim Buys a Tent

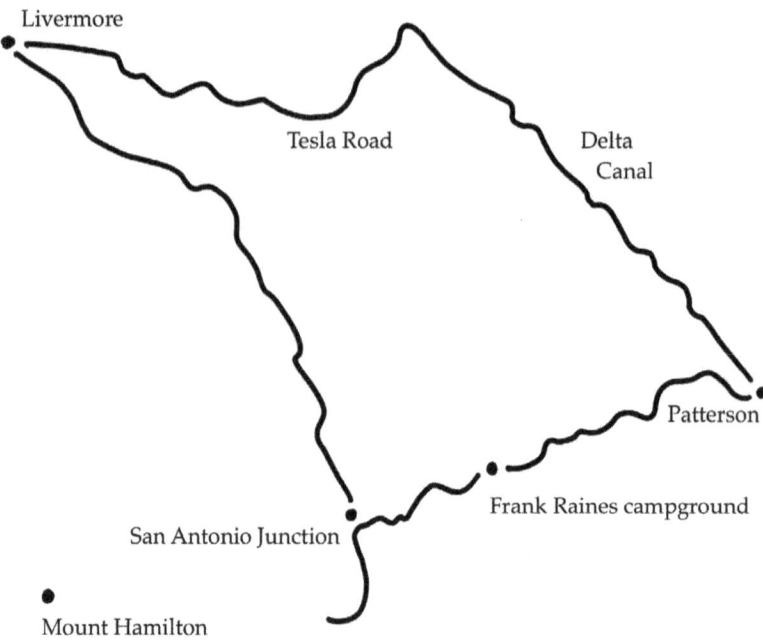

Our first solo bicycle tour in the Sacramento Valley exposed a few wrinkles in our quest to becoming Independent Bicycle Travelers. One of the hardest was the realization that California is not rural France. The hills of the Dordogne were fun but they are just that, hills. California is bigger, higher, steeper, harsher, and bolder. Cycle touring on our own home turf was more difficult than we expected.

After hours of research and tire kicking, Jim dragged me with him to check out and okay his choice of tent and sleeping bags at REI. While he will allow me a veto, I mostly trust his judgment. I know my limitations; I'm neither an equipment person nor a shopper, both bore me to tears. On the other hand, although Jim loves guidebooks, he finds maps and detailed route-planning tedious. Mr. Spontaneous prefers to just let things unfold and was happy to let me pick the routes. Slowly, we learned that we made a pretty good team and realized our good fortune at our compatibility.

Radiantly happy with his new purchases, he surprised me on the way home, "Let's test them out in Livermore. It's only an hour drive south from here. We can drive down Friday morning and come back the next day. There's a campground on the eastern side of Mount Hamilton." He remembered seeing a sign years ago, back when he was a Weekend Warrior. "Look it up, it should be a manageable distance from Livermore." A Native Californian, he knew a lot more than I did about the nooks and crannies of the East Bay.

Sure enough, Stanislaus County had a campground, Frank Raines, named after a county supervisor who died in

1953, the year the campground was dedicated to him. That says something about the guy, getting his name in lights that fast after buying the farm? Jim wanted to just head south from Livermore and ride the same route back again.

Ugh, I thought. *I'm a looper*—I always prefer to do a loop than an out-and-back. So I studied the maps some more and found the California Aqueduct/Mendota Canal in the San Joaquin Valley had an access road. I found Jim in the garage working on the bikes.

"Jim, how about we make the ride a little more interesting, make it a loop?" I suggested. "What if we went out Tesla Road to the valley? The canal has a frontage road and we can turn west at Del Puerto Canyon Road." I mumbled, "It'll add some miles, though."

"More? You want to make it longer, our first time loaded with the tent? I dunno . . ."

"Yeah, but good news: it's flatter. Mines Road climbs to 3,000 feet; the canal route is only half that."

"Half, huh? Okay, I'm game, if you say so. But it's your ass on the line."

Tesla Road was mostly isolated rundown ranches, the transition to today's (sniff) Hoity Toity Wine Country was only just beginning. The first few miles along the canal were laid back. We were on hard-packed dirt on the top of a levee with a view in all directions. To the far west was the spring-green Diablo Range we just cycled through, at the base was a strip of brown farms, and next came the bustling Interstate 5, a blur of cars and trucks racing north and south. Last was the cold blue-gray water of the California Aqueduct, with us riding on the levee. From time to time, we caught a glimpse of the parallel Mendota Canal on our left, which occasionally got within a half mile of us. Then came more farmland, and far to the east, the Sierra Nevada which lead to Lesson #6: Following the Water is Dreamy. But we found it wasn't all dreamy—after a couple of miles, we encountered a locked gate across the levee. Ugh, we had to take off all our gear, portage it over the locked gate, then load up again. And it happened four times. Although the Aqueduct flowed all the way to Southern California, we left it after twenty miles to turn west, thank goodness, stopping at a gas station in Patterson on Highway 5 for ice cream and cold drinks.

After climbing another nine miles back into the Diablo Range, we arrived at a completely empty campground just before 1 p.m. on a Friday. We set up our tent and checked out the facilities. The 1950s-era, cinderblock building was well maintained, clean, and had unlimited hot water showers; pretty posh for a county campground. Because it was still early afternoon, we decided to stash our gear in the tent and ride unloaded up the canyon to San Antonio Valley Road, noted for its fields of wild flowers, especially in spring. We knew we couldn't make it all the way to the top of Mount Hamilton, that was another thirty-five miles and four-plus hours because the climb was 4,000 feet plus. We'd try that if/when there was a next time; it would require staying two nights in the campground. This trip was a one-nighter, just to try out Jim's new tent.

We clipped along up the unpopulated valley—farmhouses were very few and far between—the fields awash in blue and violet, orange and white blooms. It was so pretty, so worth the extra miles. But we had another motive. The guidebook said there was a restaurant, the Junction Bar and Grill. Truly in the middle of nowhere, it survived on the odd ducks who made their way to this remote corner of the Bay

Area, at the junction of three roads leading to Livermore, Patterson, and Mount Hamilton. We'd packed only nonperishable food, so a restaurant meal was irresistible.

We pulled into the dusty parking lot and leaned our bikes up against the post in front of a big picture window. Even so, Jim still locked the bikes. The place wasn't too busy, the weekend crowd probably didn't start for a few more hours. There were four motorcyclists, several birders in regalia rivaling the birds' plumage, and a couple of local old-timers stopping by for news, mail, and cold beers. The long room had a huge volcanic-rock fireplace in one corner, a hammered-copper bar, and a walk-in refrigerator behind the bar covered with bumper stickers and decals put up by customers dating back decades. "Real Cowboys Don't Line Dance." "Well-Behaved Women Seldom Make History." "For kicks, see a rodeo." We ordered the American staple of burgers and fries. It was not great but not terrible. If the fries are hot and crispy and the burger pink, I'm happy. Plus the beer was on tap.

It didn't take long for an across-the-room conversation to get started. Lesson #7: Travel Cyclists Attract Mosquitoes. That's what Jim came to call the people who can't resist asking the three questions: Where are you from? Where are you going? and, How fast do you travel? Most people fall into one of two groups: the first group thinks we're crazy and wants to keep a wide berth in case we're contagious or, worse yet, ax murderers. This was a hard connection for me to understand. I mean, how many news headlines have you read that said: "Infamous cycle touring/ax murdering couple caught while trying to escape on road outa town"? The second group also thinks we're crazy but wants to know why we do this, then cure us and get us into a car or RV.

Chapter 3

The restaurant was quiet enough that when the youngest of the motorcyclists caught my eye. He asked, "Where are you going?" and everyone heard him.

Jim cringed as I answered, "Frank Raines campground." Jerry introduced himself and volunteered that they just rode over Mount Hamilton from Gilroy. Then the female birder piped up, "Oh, that campground is too noisy to enjoy." Next thing you know, someone asks, "Where are you from?" And when I say "Martinez," well, one of the bikers knows someone whose sister lives in Martinez. Jim's body language tells me he want to get out of there ASAP as the conversation starts bouncing around the room. I loved it—meeting new people and chewing the fat with strangers. Jim, not so much. He'd tolerate it as long as he either didn't have to talk too much or if he got to talk about equipment. Then he lit up. Usually, equipment talking occurred outside, standing around the bikes with comments about components.

Speaking of equipment, on a narrow hairpin turn on our way back to the campground, we came across a splayed and shattered red Ducati motorcycle in the dirt on the shoulder just past a long black skid mark. It wasn't there on the way up, that's for sure. It was totaled. We assumed someone had transported the driver to a hospital. We soberly looked at each other, reaffirming the need for care on these back roads. We never found out the story.

When we returned to the campground at 5 p.m. the place was packed—bedlam! *Every* spot was taken and filled with campers and utility vans of every size and shape imaginable. Big campers, RVs, vans, trailers. And the din of motorcycles came down from the hills just beyond the campground. The campground has a huge off-road vehicle park just adjacent. And that weekend was an annual Trial

Bike competition. The campground was filled with families. I wished I packed our camera, but it was a monstrous number, the Pentax K-1000, hard to justify carrying. Turns out, trial bikes are uniquely designed small motorcycles that don't have seats because the drivers must stand to execute the physical maneuvers. Who knew? And this competition was "fun for the whole family"—there were competitions for adults and children, boys and girls, even kids as young as four were eligible to compete, and some did.

The whole place sparkled from the sun shining on so many metallic surfaces, except for our forlorn campsite. Not one behemoth piece of machinery in it, the driveway completely empty, our two bikes locked to the end of our empty picnic table, and a tent only tall enough for sitting staked in the grass. We were embarrassed by the dramatic difference. The campsites were first-come, first-served but we somehow felt we had "stolen" a spot from a trial bike family. We were pretty much ignored as we sheepishly made our way to the showers. It was clear that except for us, everyone knew everyone; this was a big deal event that felt like a reunion.

Our campsite was near a grassy little mound that was popular with the under-four set—the kids too little to compete. Over and over again, they pushed their hot wheels up the slope, glided down and rolled over in the soft grass, which I imagine would be worn out by Sunday. Oh, I wished I had brought our camera.

Even though we had eaten, we were hungry again and laid out our pathetic spread on the picnic table: homemade sandwiches, nuts, fruit, and to compensate for the meager spread, we had a big bag of Doritos and a small bag of Pepperidge Farm cookies. Just as we were about to start eating, our neighbor, a perky blond, forty-something woman in a

Chapter 3

team T-shirt, denim shorts and sun visor carrying a steaming covered casserole, stopped, looked at us, and said, "Hey, we're having a potluck in the Pavilion. Why don't you join us?"

As Jim tried to disappear under the table, I replied, "Oh, but we don't have anything to share."

She tilted her head, rolled her eyes and said, "The kids love Doritos, and you two look like you could benefit from something more substantial. Come on over, it's a lot of fun." and hurried off.

As she walked away I turned to Jim, "Whaddya think? Should we go?" Jim gave me that look I long ago became familiar with. Cornered, he would much really rather not, would never choose to socialize with strangers, but he knew I wanted to; the invite was catnip to me. Plus, it would be churlish to say no, he knew it and I knew he knew it. I got a wickedly happy grin and clapped my hands—a party, we were invited to a party. Well, technically a potluck.

After shaping my newly opened bag of Doritos into a bowl on the potluck table, we filled (their) paper plates with their piping hot food, and sidled ourselves to a far corner table, where we could enjoy their show from a distance. It was such fun watching these enthusiastic, happy families. Ellen, the woman who invited us, stopped by. She lived not too far away in the valley, had three boys, eleven, nine, and seven, said they'd discovered trial biking through neighbors a few years ago. All five of them loved it and competed. She said their whole lives changed once they discovered trial riding. There were events year round in California and the Western states so they bought an RV and trailer to get to them. She noticed our meager plates were already empty. "Don't be shy, go back for seconds. We'll have lots of leftovers." After a lighter second serving we left early and fell asleep just past dusk to the sound of happy campers and squealing kids.

We had to cover about fifty miles the next day to get back to the car, and even with the night's lovely bonus dinner, we knew the next day's breakfast and lunch would be ho-hum, with no options for a cooked meal until we got to Livermore. At first light, we climbed out of our tent and quietly broke camp as a few early birds made their way to the facilities. We left so early none of the campers nearest us were up and out yet, but we figured within minutes of our departure, some family would fill in our campsite. As we passed the closed Junction Bar and Grill, Jim said, "For our next trip, let's buy some cooking gear, and two front panniers for me to carry it. Lightweight, of course!" My growling tummy made me realize he was right; cycling and cold food weren't a good combo. But the weight of all that stuff—there had to be some limit to what it was wise to carry.

Lovely Frank Raines campground

FOUR

Jim & Anne Go Au Naturel

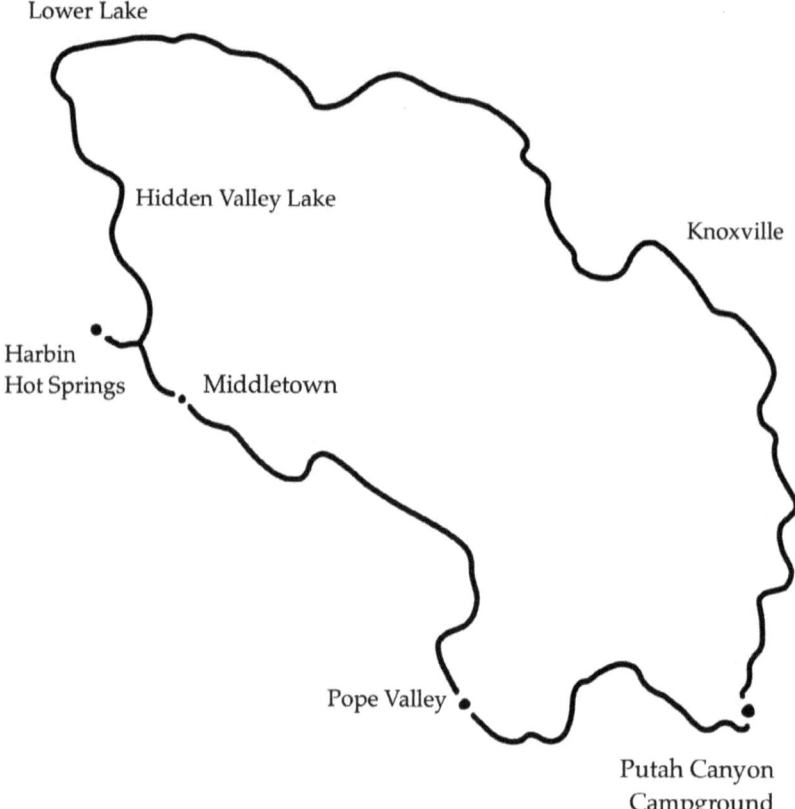

Jim found the next step of choosing the right cooking gear, quality but lightweight, more time consuming than he expected. But we had an open three-day weekend coming up and we both wanted to cycle somewhere. Where? One of our Northern California cycling guidebooks recommended the back roads on the border of Napa and Lake counties, even suggesting a place to stay overnight, Harbin Hot Springs.

Located just north of Middletown, it had campsites, a restaurant, a grocery store, and even a communal kitchen. It read like the perfect solution to our dilemma—we could cook some meals in their kitchen with groceries from their store, supplemented with dining in their restaurant, all without having to get our own cooking equipment yet. There was a hitch, though: the place was clothing optional. We had made visits to nude beaches years ago but found them too cold to enjoy on the foggy Northern California coast, even in summer. What would the place be like? What did clothing optional mean at a place with campgrounds, restaurants, and kitchens? Did people cook in the nude, dine in the nude? We really had no idea what to expect.

In the meantime, I mapped out another loop route. I found a campground, Putah Canyon, on Lake Berryessa's northern shore. We called them, explained our plans, and asked if we could camp one night and leave our car for one or two more. They said, sure, for a small extra fee. The trip started coming into focus. We'd just have to wait until we got to Harbin to see what the deal was.

We drove into the pretty, quiet Putah Canyon campground on Lake Berryessa early enough to go swimming after setting up our tent, even though it was April. Cold but doable at this lovely site created by the construction of Monticello Dam in '57.

The next morning, after a no-cook breakfast, we packed our gear, moved our car, and took off for Harbin along the Knoxville-Berryessa Road. It wasn't long before we both felt a little uneasy, just the two of us, mile after mile after mile of empty landscape that seemed devoid of human activity except for barbed wire fences and grazing cows.

My loop put us on a grueling fifty-five-mile roller coaster that left us pretty ragged by the time we arrived at Harbin. I mentally added another lesson to our list. #8: Geography is Destiny. Never underestimate the landscape's ability to awe but also to overwhelm. Cars can cover fifty-five miles with-out batting an eyelash, but this time I bit off more than we could chew.

The first twenty miles were cute, remote farms, rustic fences; by mile forty, we were feeling the workout and less entertained by the rolling hills, barns, and rusting equipment. By mile fifty-five, we were wiped and our heinies hurt. We live in such an automobile-centered, gas-powered world and there's an almost universal sense of impatience—we want it when we want it, and we want to be here NOW, not in another two hours. Jim and I slowly came to understand that the places where we pedaled didn't give a shit if/when we were ready to call it a day. The self-guided Dordogne tour was wonderful but sold us an illusion about cycle touring. As fatigued as I was I began to appreciate this uneasy lesson—my bod was sore but slowing down and solitude can be good for the soul.

We pedaled up to the check-in kiosk at Harbin and I noticed a sign that read, "If you're in a hurry, you're probably not in the right place." I was intrigued by both the message and its distinctive, unique hand-lettering.

"Good morning." said a young man with short dark hair, stubble, and a sleepy look. After checking in, we pushed our bikes up a hill past a stunning gate, a handcrafted, green-corroded dragon with a long, licking tongue and an even longer loping tail, welded to an industrial-strength steel frame. An exquisite, one-of-a-kind creation that told me we were entering a space with a genuine appreciation of all things beautiful.

Inside the gate, the road continued up to and then encircled a blue and white painted wooden gazebo with benches around a bubbling water fountain. To the east, the top floors of several low-slung, interconnected buildings descended back down the hillside. They housed the restaurant, store, library, a study, and many multi-use rooms. On the west side, a grassy flat area before the slope became steep enough to have retaining walls. The walls were remnants of rough, nineteenth-century stone construction.

One particularly high wall had a more recent, lovely glass and tile mandala. I was entranced; it was obvious an effort has been made to repair the walls, honoring the imperfections. I'd learned the habits of recycling and reusing from my thrifty, Depression-era mother, so I was intrigued. I thought *they don't throw things away here, they don't bulldoze the old to make way for the new* (like so much of California). They incorporate the old into the new, and the effect felt welcoming to me.

Back on the east side of the road, just after the community buildings that sloped down the hill, was another large grassy area shaded by enormous trees, with Adirondack chairs, and whimsical deer and Buddha statues. Several

Victorian-era buildings with wrap-around porches and rooms for overnight accommodation were adjacent.

Everywhere we roamed there were beautiful hand-lettered signs informing visitors of what was where. I was a goner. I took calligraphy in college, and oh I loved it, but it was so hard for me. I had a great teacher, but calligraphy is an art that calls for a slowed-down nature. I didn't have the patience then, but I sure could appreciate it now. *Who has made this place so beautiful, so beguiling?* I wondered.

Studying the signs, we realized we'd have to retrace our path down almost to the kiosk and go up around the east side of the canyon, past another one-of-a-kind piece of art (a round, sloped-roof building where the yoga classes were held) to get to the Meadow Campground. There were hardly any campers, maybe because we were there on a weekday in April. We chose a campsite next to the flowing Harbin Creek, with a raised wooden platform to compensate for the lack of flat terrain, for pitching tents. It didn't take us long to set ours up and stash our gear. Jim locked the bikes to a nearby tree, tarped them, and off we went to explore the pools. I could tell Jim was as intrigued as I was by all we saw, and yet so far, we hardly spoke, absorbing quietly while trying to process what we had discovered.

The footpath from the campground followed a ridge, allowing us to view the valley we had just traversed. We came around the bend and saw the pool area for the first time — the pools were just down from the main source of the springs, bubbling up at the narrowest point of the canyon. Both very hot and very cold springs filled the three main pools; the coldest was the highest up, nestled under a shaded canopy of overgrown fig trees with a serene white female Buddha keeping an eye on all who approached. The hot pool came next and was covered with a handcrafted wooden shed that had multicolored windows on the downslope side, allowing the morning sun to enter and fill the darkened space with a rainbow of colors. A cast-pewter (I'm guessing as to materials) rectangular deep-relief panel, about two feet by three feet, was shaped into dramatic waves with one large salmon bursting forth. Out of its mouth, hot water poured into the pool. I'm having a hard time doing justice to this place. You really need to see for yourself its incredible beauty. Really, you should go. The sooner the better. Just stop what you're doing and go, now! Jim'll be mad at me for telling you to go—he wants to keep the place a secret, all to ourselves. Methinks one of his fantasies is to be rich enough to buy the place and have it all to himself. What he doesn't realize is, married to me, it'd be minutes before I'd be inviting all and sundry to enjoy it with us.

Next came the warm pool, maybe twelve by twenty feet, with old handrails (probably made before the current owners took over)—a pattern of lines and circles, straight outa the '50s. I love that they kept that retro railing. And the fig trees that sprouted above the cold pool had branches so enormous they swept over the hot pool roof and provided some cover to part of the warm pool. Looking west was another steep slope upward, supported by more lovingly restored nineteenth-century stone walls, with a sign in Roman letters: Excess vs. Moderation. These three pools are the heart of the place, with hand-lettered signs asking for silence. Down the slope a ways was a swimming pool. The communal kitchen was above the changing rooms.

The whole place was pretty quiet; it felt more like a ghost town than a nudist colony. It was only at the pools that we saw the clothing-optional choice being exercised. We saw less than two dozen people as we made our way around the pool area.

As we looked around, we understood immediately why this place was clothing optional, though it's pretty much clothing optional only in the pool area. We took off our clothes, tucked them into cubbies, showered, and lowered our naked, bicycle-tanned bodies into the warm pool first. Oh, it was sublime, absolutely sublime. Our muscles were sore from the long ride, and the space was so quiet, surrounded by nature and plants and the sound of flowing water. I'm not religious, not even spiritual, but Harbin is an exultingly reverent space. Clothes in the pools would spoil the beauty of this pristine place. We got it immediately. Surrender, just Be. Be in nature. It's easier to surrender being naked. So soothing. So quieting. So enticing. So seductive. We Be goners.

We lost track of time, eventually dipping into the hot and cold pools. Soon, we were flitting back and forth among the three temperatures until we lost our bones and became noodles. This day was a Game Changer for us, a milestone. We would never be the same, all because of a Nor Cal cycling guidebook recommendation.

As we soaked, I realized how much I enjoyed people watching. Most there were singletons and couples, but of all ages, and most kept to themselves. Being fit and aware, we felt comfortable and at ease in the pool spaces, even though we were naked and vulnerable. As a connoisseur of the naked body (figure drawing), hanging out in the pools provided unlimited eye candy, I loved studying the fluid, curvy lines of each body that passed my way.

Chapter 4

* * *

When we left this wondrous place, we weren't sure if we could get on our saddles and pedal and sweat and grind our way back to our car—we were so mellow and soft. But climb on we did, and found our bodies more supple and limber thanks to the unprecedented, rejuvenating respite. We stopped for groceries in Middletown at Hardester's Market. We were told they had a great deli, so we ordered up a picnic lunch and headed out Butts Canyon Road, a shorter route back that would complete my loop. We made our way through another overlooked corner of Napa County, punctuated by the occasional ranch. Jim noticed a hubcap propped at the base of a fence, then another, and another, then a bunch arranged artistically on the fence. Suddenly, there were dozens, scores, then finally, hundreds. We stopped our bikes in front of a hub-capped gate that announced Litto's Hubcap Ranch. Turns out Litto started collecting and displaying waylaid hubcaps in the '40s. There were thousands of hubcaps, many donated over the years, even in the decades since Litto's death in the '80s. We ate our picnic lunch in the shade across the way and enjoyed the uncommon view.

An hour later, we loaded up the car and headed home. While we looked forward to continuing our cycle touring, we talked about this new, unexpected development. We agreed Harbin was a place we wanted to return to, as soon and as often as possible. I said to Jim. "Maybe we can detour to Harbin on the way home from our next Nor Cal trip. Soaking in hot springs is a great way to recover."

Jim had five weeks to settle on the best cooking gear. It would be no small feat—we'd need the lightest one-burner stove, compact pots and pans, plates, cups, and silverware. I was worried about the additional weight, but reticent to say it out loud; the fifty-five-mile ride to Harbin was the most challenging yet, without additional equipment. There was a limit to how much we could carry on our bikes—how were we going to cycle with even more stuff and still manage to enjoy doing it?

Litto's Hubcap Ranch marker

Crossing bridge-less Foley Creek on Berryessa Knoxville Road

FIVE

A Seed is Planted

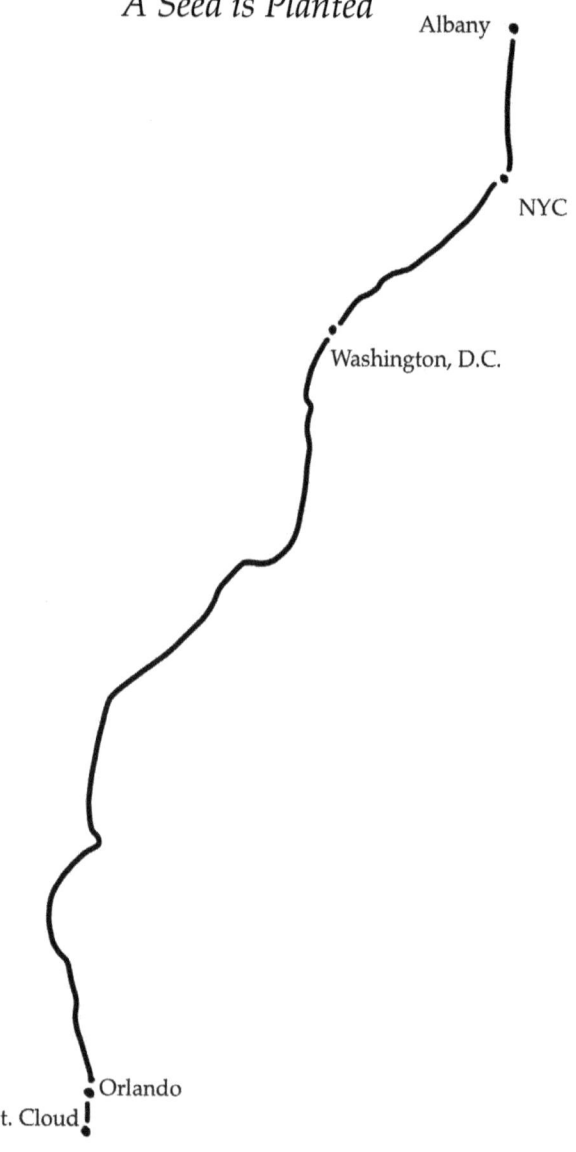

"All aboard!" My grandfather, Harvey, led my sister Mary and me, hands held super tight, up the steps and through the carpeted lounge car. "Hey, Mr. Breedlove, whatcha got there?" asked the conductor.

"Two pretty bundles," he laughed as we made our way to our seats. Harvey was friendly with all the staff on the train—the porters, attendants, conductors—and they were especially nice to us, the old retired conductor with his two young granddaughters in their Sunday best. The cars were quite spacious and lovely; wide walkways, plush upholstery, carpeting, and big picture windows. It felt like we were traveling on big, roomy, bouncy couches. Mary and I barely filled our seats. For twenty-five hours, the train carried us from New York to Orlando, Florida.

Except for a stretch in the mid-1930s, when he had to resort to driving a taxi cab to pay the bills, Harvey worked for the New York Central System railroad. He ran away from home, deep-South Alabama, in 1904 when he was 14, lied about his age, and joined the Navy in Mobile. The end of his tour of duty found him in Cambridge, Massachusetts, where he landed a conductor post on the Boston-to-Albany run, married my grandmother, Ella, and had two boys, Arthur and Daniel. A few years later, they moved to Albany, the other end of the route.

In 1955, two years after I was born, Harvey and Ella became homeowners for the first time. After decades of renting in Albany, they decided to retire, surprisingly, to the South—not the horrid South of his childhood, but to the sunny retirement South of pokey (at that time) central

Florida. They bought a very modest, 750-square-foot, two-bedroom cottage an hour's drive south of Orlando on Connecticut Avenue in the town of St. Cloud. Between the house and the attached carport was a screened-in porch where they set up two Army-surplus cots for grandkids to sleep on each summer.

It was tough for my parents, with six kids at that point and four more to come. They couldn't afford to take vacations, economically or logistically, without help. The only summer vacations they ever took were to the New Hampshire seacoast when my grandparents rented two cabins big enough for everyone. There's fun pictures, clam digging along the rocky seacoast and swimming and such, but family vacations went *poof* when Harvey and Ella left for St. Cloud in '55. So, feeling bad about deserting us, they told my parents two kids could come down every summer.

My grandfather's retirement package included train travel, so up he would come once school got out and take the kids down, then bring them home in time for the start of the new school year. My first turn came the summer of '60. I was six years old, and deemed big enough for the trip, finally. And because we were inseparable, Mary, two years younger but already taller than me, would go too. She was really too young, but everyone knew she'd be lost an entire summer without me. Also, the family was moving that summer from a two-bedroom Cape Cod cottage to a five-bedroom Sears Roebuck catalog house. With me and Mary gone, my pregnant-with-number-nine mother would find it easier to handle the prep and packing.

It was a long ride, and Harvey's perk did not include sleeper berths. Mary and I sat on facing window seats with Grandpa on the aisle. Train food was pricey, so my Mother

Chapter 5

sent us with a basket of food and drinks. At some point, Mary noticed the water fountain at the end of the car and, bored, invented a game of slipping past Harvey and making her way to the end of the car, more fascinated with turning the water on and off than drinking it. Harvey would see her go, wag his finger and scold her to come back, but the scolding only energized her further.

The landscape slowly changed as we made our way south. The trees and vegetation stayed familiar for a good ways, and New Jersey and Pennsylvania felt the same as New York. Once we crossed the Mason-Dixon Line (though I had no idea that's what we were doing), we were going through a place like nothing I had ever seen before. The South looked and felt very different. Massive trees draped with Spanish moss cast deep shade in the sultry heat I could see and feel through the train window. Occasional glimpses of far off, stately mansions with wrap-around porches could be seen through the trees. Old wooden billboards advertised unfamiliar sodas like Mountain Dew and Dr Pepper.

One sees a very different world on a train. Riding in a car or a bus, it's like walking in the front door of someone's home; on a train, it's like entering through the back door. While the train goes deep in and out of the heart of a city, it goes behind all the pretty buildings, homes, and parks. It's a grittier view, through the rougher and poorer parts of the cities, towns, and countryside. The houses along the tracks were often flimsy, ramshackle numbers, with yards of hard-packed dirt devoid of much greenery. Shoeless, half-naked kids stopped playing in their barren yards to watch me go by on the train as I watched them at play, entranced.

Once we arrived in Orlando, Harvey led us to his parked blue and white '56 Chevy for the final twenty-five-mile drive on a dusty, lonely, one-lane road. We looked a sight. I mean, after twenty-five hours nonstop on the train plus the drive in the car, my Grandmother Ella immediately put Mary and I in the tub. Back then, dressing was quite different from today—we left home in starched, ironed dresses.

Everything about that summer was idyllic to me. The adventure, the escape, the ratio! Just us two kids with our two grandparents, versus ten-to-two at home, all summer long. What's not to love? We slept on cots in the porch off the kitchen. Curiously, my grandparents each had their own room, with their own double bed. Ella had a trundle sewing machine in her room that she would let us pump on our hands and knees while she pretended to sew. The kitchen was so tiny they built a collapsible two-person table on hinges that could be folded down to make space for cooking.

There was only one communal room where we ate on a plastic-lace-covered table at the end closest to the kitchen. On the wall above the table was an ancient, oval-framed and hand-colored photo of two-year-old "Baby Brother," as the family called my father's little brother, Daniel, who died during the 1918-1920 flu pandemic, shortly before the family moved to Albany to try to escape the memories.

Their cottage sat in the front of a long, narrow yard with an alley at the back for service trucks. They had citrus trees and huge succulents with flowers bigger than Mary and I. Harvey operated a wringer washing machine just outside the back porch door, and Ella hung the wash on diagonally staked poles. When she filled them with sheets, we used them to play hide-and-seek. Harvey bought some two-by-fours and made us stilts—oh, the hours we played on them—clomping like mini-giants around their yard.

Chapter 5

Some days, it was fun just to lay on our backs in the scratchy Bermuda grass and watch the clouds. Big, bulbous, ever-changing forms; we turned it into a game, trying to name the shapes as they morphed. Rabbit, duck, face, frog, cloud, over and over again. It rained every day, mostly in the afternoon, but rarely for more than ten or twenty minutes. Occasionally, it poured so intensely the sandy street flooded with rainwater and turned into a pond until the drainage system could process the volume. Sometimes, when the danger of lightning wasn't too great, we were allowed to run and splash in the temporary pond.

Ten long blocks away was East Tohopekaliga Lake where my grandparents would take us to swim. I don't ever remember them getting in the water with us. Surprising, considering how good it felt to jump in and get relief from the humidity.

They would set up their lounge chairs and umbrellas and relax in the shade while we swam. Even the lake was different, we swam off a sandy beach inside an area bigger than a football field, enclosed by U-shaped chain-link fencing anchored in the sandy bottom and rising several feet above the water level. The fence was to keep the alligators out of the swimming hole. I'm incredulous that my grandparents were comfortable letting us swim on our own in a lake infested with 'gators—fence or no fence.

Twice more, Mary and I spent the summer with Harvey and Ella in St. Cloud. There were so many of us at home and only one car that we kids lived a fairly confined, pedestrian existence centered around an insular, Catholic parish school run by the Sisters of Mercy. My childhood neighborhood conjures up mostly black-and-white images. Florida was a colorful antidote.

After my third summer with them, I kept up my connection with Harvey and Ella through letters. When my firstborn was old enough, I shared my love of trains with him: Brio trains, Oshkosh coveralls, and Amtrak trips to the Sacramento train museum. Harvey mailed me his cherished New York Central System Conductor Manual a few years before he passed away in 1985 at the age of 94. I keep it on the bookshelf next to my bed. When I open it, I see his handwriting and can smell the cigar he smoked each evening as he sat in his rocking chair in the cottage, alongside a cold can of beer. It was with Harvey on the train that I first developed a taste for travel and adventure.

Harvey and his wringer washer

Harvey and Ella on their 50th wedding anniversary

My sister Mary and I on our first trip to St. Cloud

SIX

Jim and Anne Get Lost

Looking back, I can see one of the things Jim and I did right was to take things slow. In 2009, five months into our second big post-retirement trip, cycling across Australia, we were deep in the Outback when we met a young man from Perth who decided his first cycle tour would be crossing the Nullarbor—the vast stretch of desolate dessert in the middle of the continent—and by himself, no less. All beat up and discouraged, he threw in the towel on day three, hitched a ride with a road train (an Aussie tractor-trailer that has not one, not two, but *three* trailers), and decided cycle travel was not for him. Really? Already? *Too soon*, I wanted to tell him. We felt sad for him. Maybe if we had been dumb enough to take on a route way beyond our reach early on we, too, would have backed out permanently. But as it happened for us, and most definitely not that we planned it, but more by sheer luck—and fear actually, we slowly built up our skill set and equipment in manageable steps that didn't kill our interest. I cannot emphasize how important and lucky we were in that respect.

We bit off a bit more on our next trip, going from our Harbin frolic to Humboldt's Lost Coast, but the beauty and isolation of the landscape would prove to soft-pedal (pun intended) the physical challenges, especially after our return (kinda like childbirth, for those of you with experience in that vein, the memory of the hardest parts soften over time). But I'm getting ahead of myself.

An important first for this trip: While I kept a journal on our '77 honeymoon and our '97 cycle tour of the Dordogne, it hadn't occurred to me to pack a journal for our cycle trips, maybe because I was focused on carrying the bare minimum. In the course of our first three rides, I realized Jim is a pokey-puppy—whatever we are doing always takes him longer. So I end up sitting around, twiddling my thumbs, and then—voilà, lightbulb moment. I started packing a journal and a sketch pad into my handle bar bag.

We parked at Humboldt Redwoods State Park and had forty miles to that night's camping. The ride up the frontage road along 101 through the dense, redwood forest was dark and damp and delicious. We experienced a curious change when we entered the tidy, bucolic town of Scotia; it was just adorable. Every house was in pristine shape, painted with happy, vibrant colors—like the way San Francisco's Painted Ladies appear in postcards. The entire town felt out of place; it felt more like Disneyland than NorCal. Then, we crossed the Eel River and entered Rio Dell, and—instantaneously—went from Total Tidiness to Rundown Rural Trashiness. Striking transition. Gosh, it's such an education to see rural America up close. Turns out, Pacific Lumber Company wholly owns and maintains Scotia while Rio Dell has to make do in the post-lumber economy. And it shows. It was only the first of many such disconcerting juxtapositions we would experience pedaling the rural parts of Northern California, and later the US.

We stopped for groceries in the scenic Victorian town of Ferndale, where we did a little bit of sightseeing and picked up a couple of bottles of wine (not the smartest choice with the climbing ahead, but Jim wanted to enjoy the evenings). We made our way through some abundantly fertile farmland at the mouth of the Eel River to Centerville Beach County Park. A county park, but *sans* campground. There was no reasonable camping options the right distance from the car, they were either too close or too far. So, we decided to free-camp on the beach, waiting for most everyone to leave before we set up our tent. Some call it guerrilla or stealth camping but I prefer *free*, popular with more committed cycle tourists, and would soon become my favorite way to end a day. Cycle all day then push the bikes off the road into the forest, set up camp, make a cup of tea, write and sketch, and let Jim cook dinner (he is a far better cook than I).

We pushed our bikes through soft sand — ugh — almost a mile down the coast, to get away from the parking lot, and settled in a notch at the base of the cliff, where we could hardly be seen, up against enormous driftwood logs with little yellow-orange and white wildflowers in its cracks. Jim inaugurated the one-burner WhisperLite stove, propping it on top of a flat driftwood log to keep it out of the sand, and the sand out of it. He cooked no-longer-frozen shrimp and a box of jambalaya rice mix in our new Teflon two-pot set. Tiny but serviceable. It's tough to be so hungry when we have such limited options, especially as we could smell the steaks being grilled nearby. Jim was right, the wine took away some of the pain of our meager meal. The horses and surfers left while we were cooking, the sunset watchers took a bit longer, and a few stuck around and built fires in the dark. It was a lovely, sunny, windless evening in spite of going to bed still a little hungry and we finished off a bottle before climbing in the tent.

The mood changed dramatically come morning. We unzipped the door to the tent into a howling wind. The free-camping part of the night worked out fine, the sandy beach part, not so much. And I yearned for a picnic table to put under our new red-and-white checked REI plastic tablecloth. Instead, I had to settle for trying to keep it flat on the sand in the wind. Trying to cook oatmeal on a beach in that wind was a mistake, big mistake. Even the coffee ended up with sand in it. We should have just had cold coffee and bagels with peanut butter in the tent. Learning as we go.

The Lost Coast is a stretch of Humboldt county that is hard to get to, hard to get through, and hard to get out of your system once you hang there for a while. It's the least developed section of the entire California coast; the fewest roads, fewest towns, lowest population, and the most incredible forests. Hence: Lost. The getting in and out requires going up and over some pretty steep ridges of the King Range, including dirt stretches that have never been paved because they are too steep for the machinery to pave them. That brings up Lesson #9: Which is Worse? Really a version of Pick Your Poison, both choices were going to hurt. Keep pedaling up a ridiculously steep stretch with screaming thighs OR stop and walk, knowing that remounting the bike won't happen until the road flattens out again with no idea when that's gonna happen. I'm guessing this is not the easiest thing for a non-cyclist to picture, but suffice it to say, it's a tough call—the next flat-enough stretch to remount my loaded bike might be right around the corner, or it might be miles ahead—which means a lotta walking and pushing.

Out of the frying pan and into the fire. We got away from the wind, but once we turned south, we hit the first of many steep grades.

"I've gotta walk." I yelled to Jim, who was quite a ways back. As he caught up to me, I huffed, "You don't have to walk on my account." Jim did his best to go as slow as he could and stay behind me, but he eventually passed me. Me, I'm huffing and puffing and cursing under my breath, sending Evil Eye Darts, wishing him to fall. Finally, he dismounted, and I felt bad for getting mad at him. After several miles of alternatively cycling and pushing, we crested at 2,000 feet, and the view made up for the pain. Blue sky and ocean as far as we could see. We had made our way through primordial forests to an even more remote coastline, alternating stretches of damp, drizzling forest and wide-open parched grassland. Jim stopped several times to collect seeds to try to germinate at home.

We dropped down to Capetown, a three-house hamlet, and stopped for a picnic lunch on the banks of the Bear River. A path leading down to the water just over the bridge lead to a rocky beach that had a picnic table. We could see the bridge, only a few farm vehicles crossed while we ate. They could see us, but no one came down to check us out. After lunch, we had to climb back up to 1,000 feet because the Bear River came all the way down to sea level, but on top, we again found ourselves on a grassy bluff overlooking a sunlit coast.

We rode our brakes down another steep slope as we dropped back down to Black Sand Beach. "Look," cried Jim, "Cape Mendocino lighthouse, the westernmost point in the continental US." To the north, we could see the red-roofed, small old lighthouse standing over the cliff with a rickety white fence leading down to the water. It was just stunning and so energizing; putting out so much physical effort and then ending up at a place as splendid as this. Then, for five miles, we coasted along a flat, straight stretch of asphalt hugging the beach. It was exquisite, the surf pounding the sand mere yards from us. Not a car in sight, just us two feeling like our bikes had motors. Blue water, brown sand, and gray rocks on one side, golden yellow grasses and purple lupine dancing in the wind on the other.

When we pulled into the scrappy little town of Petrolia, we encountered another first: a loaded-cycle tourist, a twenty-something young man pulling a trailer instead of panniers. We slowed to a stop.

"Hey," Jim said, "how's it going?"

"Not too bad, heading to San Francisco. How about you?" It was fun to compare notes, the first of many times we would stop on the side of the road and commiserate with members of Our Tribe over the joys and tortures of cycle touring, giving and getting tips for the road ahead. In this instance, Jim led the conversation, so intrigued was he with Fred's equipment. Another pattern established: Jim brakes for equipment.

"I'm gonna go in and get ice cream, you guys want one?" I asked.

"Sure," Jim and Fred piped up simultaneously. Gave them more time to talk shop. We could afford to laze around, it was only six more miles to our next campground, a tiny, bare-bones number—no potable water, only pit toilets—run by the Bureau of Land Management where the Mattole River joined the ocean. We got there early enough in the afternoon to swim in the river (in our cycling clothes to try to wash away our two-day stink). We cooked a meatless (it wouldn't have kept) spaghetti (note to self: macaroni is way easier to cook in a tiny pot.) accompanied by a bottle of red as we heard kids yelling and playing in the sand, a neighboring camper singing to his guitar, and the smells of car-camping dinners more luxurious than ours.

* * *

In another lost town, Honeydew, the store cashier told me their K-8 school had less than thirty students. The mom-

and-pop shop inspired Lesson #10: The Smaller the Store, the Crummier the Food. We needed to pay attention and get good food when we could. Do not, I repeat, *do not* pass up good stores when you see them, regardless the time of day. Rural stores are guaranteed to carry junk: snacks, cigarettes, and liquor, and not much else Not paying attention can result in going to bed hungry.

The next day, we climbed back over the King Range through thick redwood forest, arriving at the posh (compared to the previous campsites) Albee Creek State Park with coin-operated hot showers, a real luxury. Though it was raining the following morning, I insisted we bike to Dyerville Road to check out the two thousand-year-old Dyerville Giant, a majestic redwood beauty I had read about in *The Chronicle,* that fell during a storm in 1991. We quietly walked its length, 362 feet, and hung out at the trailhead long enough to down a thermos of hot soup to warm us up for the ride back to our car.

I calculated we averaged five mph this trip, twenty-eight hours of cycling 144 miles over four days. I so wanted to know the total elevation climb. This was the beginning of my addiction to data. Eventually, Jim selected the Garmin eTrex Vista, a chunky little black-and-silver number, about two by four inches and an inch thick, with a screen only about an inch square. He installed it on my handlebar and I soon couldn't live without it, quickly becoming a total data junkie, tracking miles, elevation, hours, etc.

We detoured to Harbin on the drive home and the place was hoppin' with, of all things, a five-day Pagan Festival. It takes all kinds to make a world. We steered clear of their "events," but couldn't miss them in the pools. Lots of rings in the most unusual of places. I won't go into tattoos—do not get me started on tattoos. And there seemed to be a strong proclivity for the Neolithic Venus look among the pagan women. And after only two visits to Harbin I can tell, yeah, breasts come in a much greater variety of sizes and shapes than penises.

The part of the ride that was the most enticing, that five-mile stretch along the coast, went by the quickest. On the way home, we agreed we wanted to do it again, but spend a night there. Lesson #11: The Best Parts of a Day's Ride Lasts the Least Amount of Time. We spent hours mounting the various ridges, and then minutes along that beautiful coast. We returned the next month and rode the loop again with a sublime night of free-camping on Black Sand Beach, accompanied only by the patterned flickering of the lighthouse. And we brought wine.

BLM campground on the Mattole River

Free camping on Centerville Beach

View of the Lost Coast

SEVEN

Lavaland

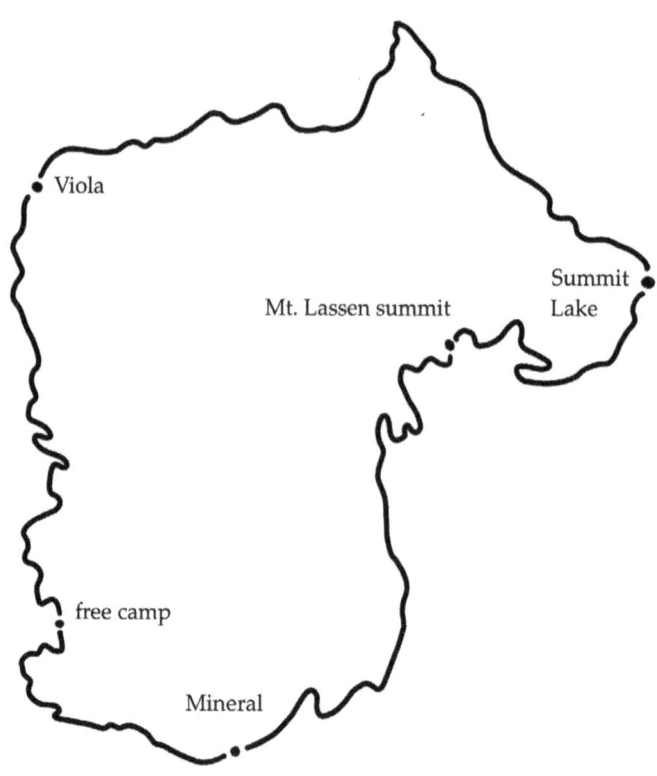

When we drove into the busy parking lot of Lassen National Park headquarters in the town of Mineral there were so many cars and trucks coming and going, I worried they'd say "No room" to my pitch to park. Jim stayed in the car. A no-nonsense ranger came out the front door as I climbed the stairs.

"Oh, excuse me," I blurted out, "Can you help us?" She looked me up and down and checked out the car with the bikes on the roof while listening to my well-rehearsed spiel.

"How long you want to do this for?" she asked skeptically. When I assured her only three days, she scanned the lot. "In the far corner, park facing out. I'll let my staff know."

Thanks, Boss, I thought as I skipped back to Jim.

You know by now I'm a sucker for a loop—riding circles turns me into a kid on a merry-go-round. As we took the bikes down I suggested to Jim, "Instead of an out-and-back, let's do a loop by taking County Road 17 north and then riding south through the park on the Scenic Volcanic Highway."

On a lovely, sunny Friday afternoon in late August, we turned away from the comfort of asphalt onto a severely washboarded and poorly maintained county dirt road that soon felt like the middle of nowhere. The first half was actually within the national park boundary, and so there really was nothing there, nothing but nature. We saw no cars before we called it a day after a couple of hours of bumpy pedaling. The Lassen Loop was the fifth trip in our Can We Travel the World by Bicycle? experiment, but we were well on our way to coining all sorts of lingo and sayings to make sense of what we did, saw, and experienced. A *hamlet* was the terminology we came up with for a place big enough to have a both a dot and a name on a map, two items that enticed us into believing there would be something there. Lesson #12: To Be a Town, Ya Gotta Have Our Big Three. A town had to have what we craved: a grocery store, a restaurant, a library. Hamlets were large enough to have dots on the map and a few buildings but not much else. When we started out, we had no idea how big a deal it was to find any of these three enterprises. By this trip, we knew.

Another dynamic we learned by this trip was that we each handled the unknown a bit differently. Jim didn't care about maps, loved to just take off and see what happened — until shit happened, then he'd start snarling about "poor planning" or, worse yet, poor map reading. Me? I never met a map I didn't like. Having been trained as a printer, I absorb things graphically. I found comfort in a map, giving me an idea of where and how we were going, what to expect. But maps and reality didn't always reconcile. Maps never adequately convey elevation change, for example. And they also only hint at road-surface quality or usage. Jim was extraordinarily anxious about traffic, so I tried to pick less-frequented roads. Sometimes, like this day, that put us feeling like we were the only humans on the planet, and in a place like Lassen, Jim soon started to worry about bears.

Whenever I get particularly nervous about bears, I start singing. This was a new thing I started on the Lost Coast, because a guidebook said one of the best defenses against bears is to make noise so they aren't surprised; they hear you first and hopefully, run away. Jim bought two bear bells that we hung from Velcro loops on our handlebars, but it wasn't enough for me. I decided to print out some lyrics, singing and memorizing them as we pedaled. The first batch was from my Cole Porter piano book: "Night and Day," "C'est Magnifique," "I Love Paris," "In the Still of the Night." I trimmed them down to business card size and slipped them into the corners of my plastic map holder. By day's end, I had a new pattern established.

We saw no cars since we'd been on the dirt road, but Jim insisted on pushing our bikes all the way across a field that felt like it must have been a bog during the rainy season. As this was late August, it was bone dry and mercifully free of mosquitoes. I stopped.

"No," Jim insisted, "We've got to get to the edge of the forest. Period. Not negotiable." I knew he was serious when he said *not negotiable*—that's MY line. If he was using it, he meant it. So I kept pushing to where the field met the forest.

"It's worth it," he said when we stopped. "It'll be less likely anyone will see us from the road." I slept well that night, knowing that none of the six million cars Jim was certain would blaze past during the night would notice our forlorn little tent in the dark. Even though we each had a can of bear spray in our tent pocket closest to the door, Jim was on edge the entire night. He had a hard time sleeping. Me? I figured he worried enough for both of us. I tended to worry more during the day as we traveled through new, unknown terrain. Once we settled down, my worries melted away. Jim was the opposite; he reveled in the spontaneity of riding through places for the first time, but when the tent was up, he became the "protector of the mansion," so to speak. So, I sang during the day to calm my anxiety and slept like a baby. Jim reveled in the newness of things during the day and spent the night imagining dire sounds and their consequences.

I woke up early, keen to get started. This is when the camp stove became an item of great reverence for me. It was far too dangerous to start open campfires in the wild. Our tiny, one-burner stove became the equivalent of a campfire hearth. Another pattern emerged. As an early riser, I came to love having a hot cup of coffee or tea to take the edge off the crisp cold air. As a result, I was usually the one to get our morning "fire" going. Coffee first, boil more water to fill our thermos with hot soup for lunch, then usually it was oatmeal or scrambled eggs. A cold breakfast just would not do. Scrambled eggs fueled us much longer in the morning than oatmeal, but there was a limit to how many we could carry—it was too horrible to discover our eggs broken in the panniers. We usually had eggs the first morning of a trip and oatmeal for the rest unless we hit a grocery store.

An hour-and-a-half later, fired up on breakfast, we flew along the northern half of the county road and returned to asphalt at yet another hamlet, Viola. Pretty place, not much there, it had none of our Big Three. Before long, we turned back into the park and entered a volcanic wonderland. Along a shady stretch of road thick with pine trees, we spied our first red, succulent, bottle-brushy flower—a bright red tubular thing poking like a penis out of a sea of browned pine needles. As we climbed toward the summit, we became surrounded by the majesty of the glacier-scraped rocks at this southernmost part of the Cascade Range.

On our second night, we upgraded: civilized camping in a bona fide campground, Summit Lake South. Again, we were the only ones without a vehicle in our parking spur. That night, we made another discovery, an exasperating and repeating nuisance. We were amazed at the number of late arrivals at car-based campgrounds, coming in after dark and struggling—duh—to find their campsite. As our site had no car in the spur, our site was a magnet for those assuming—hoping?—our spot was their spot, often resulting in headlights shining into our tent. Not so bad if it happened before we went to sleep, but that night, we had cars pull in, twice, waking us.

We stopped to take a pic next morning at the highest point on the highway—right next to the marker that said 8,511 feet—celebrate that we made it, enjoy the view, and have a bite to eat. As I was pouring out hot soup from the thermos, we were chatted up by two Mosquitoes, a term coined by Jim for strangers who just couldn't resist making contact with such an odd apparition—us. These Mosquitoes were an older couple in a Whale (another term Jim coined, the name he gave all large RVs or motor homes, often with older, unpredictable drivers). We feared the Whales, did our best to keep a maximum distance, and wished them to always pass us as quickly and seamlessly as possible. That was pretty much our attitude with all motor vehicles, and by this trip, we had developed a system. For us there, were three major types of motorists:

The Drama Queens. These people can't believe they've come upon something, anything, other than a genuine motorized vehicle, and immediately get their panties in a twist that they now have to slow down to the speed limit to pass us. Usually, as they do, they swing their vehicles all the way into the opposing lane and gun their engines, just to make sure we know they think we are a pain in the ass in their otherwise tranquil lives.

The Stephen Kings. Those who are so terrified by the appearance of such an odd occurrence—bicycles—that they freeze with terror and become almost incapable of movement, though they keep their foot on the gas pedal enough to maintain forward momentum right behind us. But the shock renders them otherwise senseless for some not-inconsiderable length of time. Sometimes, it could be upward of five minutes before they regain their senses. In the meantime, they are lingerers, shadows, hanging off and behind us, their motors purring, as we wait and wait and wait for them to just pass us already and free us from misery. Eventually, they snap out of it and finally muster the gumption to pass us, although this in itself can often add several more minutes as they wait for the perfect opportunity to pass, usually a stretch of road that is perfectly straight, perfectly flat, and has no oncoming traffic for at least a half mile. And about half of them add the gunned-engine flourish of the Drama Queens.

Finally, there's the Been-There, Done-Thats. These guys have some experience with bicycles, which means they have ridden a bicycle at least once in their lives, therefore, they can put themselves in our shoes, realize we are not a danger to them as long as they pass us prudently and expeditiously, giving us an appropriate six feet of space, and at the speed limit or just an teensy bit over. Often, I'll give them a wave or a thumb's up as they pass. (I want them to know that we know that they know, and thank them for knowing.)

Jim had a strong belief that if we were to be hit by a moving vehicle, it would more likely be from behind, so he insisted I go first. By this time, we also knew that I loved anything to do with a map and he didn't. Jim bought me a clear, snap-on map holder for my handlebar bag, and I became *La Navigatrice*. I love everything about maps, certainly the information, but also the details, colors, icons, legends, and even the folds. Yeah, you read that right, the folds. Any

CHAPTER 7   73

True Respecter of mapmaking pays attention to and honors the folds by returning a map to its original state after each use. This is very important. I'm willing to mangle, mark up, and highlight a map for getting us from point A to point B, but once the trip is over, I can't rest until my maps are returned to their original pre-use folds. And I can tell; a map incorrectly folded will be poofy in the wrong places. Poofiness is all well and good in some instances, but not on a map being laid to rest after a hard day's work.

So while we tried to enjoy our warm soup, we did our best to ignore the Whale that pulled in after us. Within minutes, however, the couple (he reminded me of Steve Buscemi and she of Debra Winger) moseyed on over and she started in with The Three Questions:

"Hi, where are you from?"

"Martinez."

"Where are you going?"

"Now? Well, actually heading back to our car in Mineral," Jim said.

"How fast do you travel?"

"If we're lucky, ten miles an hour," I politely answered while ignoring Jim's churlishness, but when she said, "I feel sorry for you, having to look down all day long, you miss all the great things to see." I had to pause before replying.

"Quite the contrary, one of the pleasures of ten miles per hour is being able to see and appreciate the details of the landscape as we travel." I then suggested she try to make out the lovely clusters of yellow wildflowers at our feet as she flew by at sixty mph. She wouldn't be able to do it, I said, she could only see the big landscape; details were a blur. She didn't seem to care for being contradicted. She turned on her heels and walked away without another word. Jim was thrilled, and unless another Whale showed up, we could enjoy our hot soup.

Jim loathed Mosquitoes more than I loathed mosquitoes. Alas, I must reveal to you that my husband is a misanthrope as well as a hermit. Opposites attract, that's for sure. It was paradoxical; his preferred method of waltzing through this world is with as little contact as possible with almost every other species on the planet, and yet here he was traveling the equivalent of a circus barker bellowing, "Come on in." Try as he might to be left alone, traveling on a bicycle loaded down with gear is a surefire way to attract attention. So I found myself, over and over again, in situations where I welcomed chatting with strangers while Jim would turn away grumpy.

We got back on our bikes and coasted a short distance to the sulfur-spewing ponds on the south flank of the volcano. There were elevated walkways over some of the swampy parts, but neither of us were tempted. First, Jim was reluctant to leave the bikes unattended, and second, we didn't want to get any closer to the foul-smelling vapors than we already were.

And then we hit upon one of the most delightful stretches of road we've ever, ever, *ever*, cycled. Many ass-kicking roads stand out, but this one was downie perfection. No surprise there as our parked car was about 3,000 feet lower, but this stretch of the Volcanic Highway had brand-new asphalt and a shallow grade with long, long straightaways, punctuated with gentle turns. We coasted at a speed that meant we didn't have to either ride our brakes or pedal. It was a six-mile carnival ride, an effortless descent through the forest with a gentle breeze and a pleasant temperature, no rain, no wind.

CHAPTER 7   75

We pulled into the closed-on-Sundays headquarters to our forlorn little blue station wagon sitting among all those big park service trucks. Fortunately, there was no locked gate across the entrance. After loading our bikes and gear, we piled our sweaty but exhilarated bodies into the car and headed south to first find somewhere good to eat—maybe Black Bear Diner in Willows (if we were really hungry) or a little further to Granzella's in Williams (if we could be patient)—and then make our way to Harbin for a well-earned soak.

Misty view of Mt. Lassen

Verdant view of Mt. Lassen

Mt. Lassen summit

Free camping on County Road 17

EIGHT

If the World Hands You Lettuce, Make a Salad

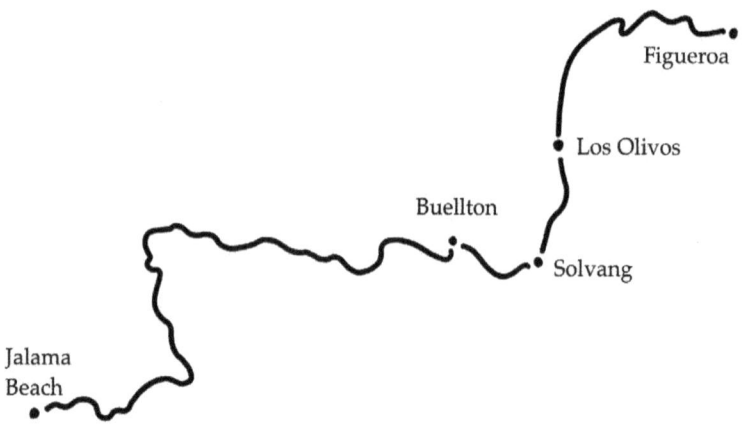

Jim spent most of his childhood in San Diego. One hot September evening while starting dinner, he turned to me.

"You know the weather is a lot milder down south. We should consider it for a ride this fall."

"How about the five days before Thanksgiving, Saturday to Wednesday?" I asked as I uncorked a bottle of Two Buck Chuck.

"Oh," Jim mused as he took the bottle from me and poured out the wine. "Maybe we can skip Thanksgiving and ride nine days?"

"Hilarious, nice try." I cut that off as I plunked ice cubes into my wine glass.

"There's some interesting agricultural valleys on the coast north of LA. Check them out."

"Okay, but remember, we have to think about daylight, or the lack of it. Daylight Savings Time will have ended, we'll be lucky if it's still light at 5:30. We'll have much less time to ride, and we'll have a lot more time in the tent."

"Maybe we should just stay in hotels?"

"We still have to carry the gear for insurance." I replied, "That's a good idea, though, if we start and stop in a hotel it'll be easier to get started and head home."

I settled on the odd-sounding town of Buellton for our anchor point, right on the freeway, close to both mountains and beach, at a hotel called Pea Soup Andersen's. What's not to love? When I called to book a room for two nights, I pitched it to the reservation agent to let us leave our car in their lot for four days in between the two nights and she said "okay."

Waking in a bright and toasty hotel room on a cold Saturday morning made it so much easier to get up and out. We arrived at the tarted-up town of Solvang before it was really awake—except for the bakeries. We stopped at the first place we saw, Olsen's, walking into a warm and sunny space, all beiges, oranges, and reds. Jim came in with me because it was really cold and he could see the bikes out the big front window.

Solvang, settled by the Danes in the early twentieth century, is a quirky kinda place, as tidy as Switzerland, a big windmill on the main drag, and lots and lots of post-and-beam buildings—with the walls and wood beams in brightly contrasting colors. Red is the dominant color throughout a town that feels like Disneyland.

"*God morgen!*" an older woman behind a huge glass display case filled with delicious-looking pastries smiled at us. "What would you like?"

"Coffee, for starters," I said.

"How do you say *apricot* in Danish, and do you have it?" Jim asked without skipping a beat

"*Abrikos*, and yes," she said. Then, "Where are you from, and where are you going?" Jim picked up the two self-serve coffee cups to fill as I answered her and continued the conversation. I also bought a beautiful loaf of Scandinavian cardamon bread (to turn into French toast, as long as our eggs didn't break). We savored the yummy Danishes and hot coffee, then blasted out of town before the hordes of weekend/holiday tourists descended.

By now, we knew we looked forward to certain things: Jim loved running into anything having to do with geology or astronomy, and I loved learning about the history of a place, stopping at libraries, visitor centers, and chambers of

Chapter 8

commerce. And we loved surprises. One of our first this trip was the manzanita plants on the climb through Los Padres National Forest—not just shrubs, but quite large, gnarly trees, distinctive because of their red-orange wood. A few miles shy of the campground in a flat, dusty clearing on the side of the road sat two telescopes, a big eight inch and smaller six-inch refractor, pointing to the sky. As we slowed down, a scruffy ponytailed man in jeans and an oversized shirt with a salt-and-pepper beard came out of the shade and said, "Hey, like the 'scopes?"

"I'm a volunteer for the Santa Barbara Astronomical Unit," he said, "setting up viewing for anyone who hopes to catch the annual Leonid meteor showers tonight. Camping up ahead? You're welcome back, of course, if you can get down here after dark." We were at a disadvantage; several miles between the campground the the scopes. Alas, Jim would have hung around longer, but we had to get moving. Our stop for breakfast and for lunch in the cute little town of Los Olivos slowed us down; we needed to finish our climb and get our tent set up before dark.

Within minutes of finishing dinner, the dark and cold drove us into the tent. Tonight, we were looking forward to going in early. Jim bought two legless "chairs" for us to sit more comfortably in the tent. The virtually weightless nylon sleeves were designed to hold our inflatable mattresses in an L-shape, softening our butts on the ground and letting us lean back—new equipment for the long hours sitting in the tent. Pile into the tent we did, putting on multiple layers and sitting in our legless chairs, our legs tucked in our our sleeping bags, and Jim's curly hair grazing the ceiling. It was getting down into the forties that night. Jim bought another new invention—Petzls—flashlights attached to elastic straps that wrapped around our heads for hands-free lighting. Jim really was great at finding tools that made touring more pleasurable.

There we were—6:30 p.m., burrowed and cocooned into our home-away-from-home probably until sunrise except to use the facilities. Jim always brought one of his favorite textbooks—usually geology, French, or astronomy because he didn't want to run out of reading material. Me, I carried a bunch of stuff: a writing journal, a sketching journal, pens, pencils, markers, guidebook, and maps.

Our new Sierra Designs tent had pockets on the sides where I could sort my "girls"—on this count, I was very clear with Jim—his stuff, his "boys," stayed on his side of the tent, and my girls stayed on mine. He had his idiosyncrasies and I had mine, so he did his best to tolerate this one. I was so particular about this separation that when he picked out the next tent, I insisted it have two doors—one for him and one for me.

That first long, cold night in the tent was fun, actually. We had the second half of our dinner bottle of wine to share (and help keep us warm, though it meant we'd have to climb out of the tent twice that night). By this trip, I realized I never had time to read for pleasure, I preferred the maps and guidebooks. I happily spent my free hours bouncing from writing and drawing to maps and guidebooks. We took turns interrupting each other lost in thought, and it became a game to see who would give up the ghost soonest, though usually it was me. I'm the early bird, Jim's the night owl; he could easily stay up an hour or two longer, especially if he was particularly enthralled with the book he brought. And come morning, I was most often the one to roll out first and get some water boiling.

Chapter 8

Next morning, we turned our gaze from the high, cold mountains out to the sea level coast, the maps showed that further east into the National Forest there was a whole lot a nothing. We weren't capable of carrying four days of food, so I picked a route that would take us past a grocery store or two. My new guidebook said there was a highly recommended Santa Barbara County campground, Jalama Beach. Having grown up a couple of blocks from tide pools, the beach was about as close to religion as Jim got.

So, we coasted down the mountain in one-tenth of the time it took us to climb up, stopping for real coffee (we carried instant) and bagels in a still-sleepy Los Olivos. Then we took a hillier alternate route that avoided Solvang, and stopped for fresh meat and more eggs near Lompoc. So close to Santa Barbara, and yet so far, we traversed a quiet valley of rolling green hills punctuated by long stretches of flat farmland, enriched by the Santa Ynez River as it snaked its way west to the coast. The smell of fertile dirt filled the air as we pedaled past recently harvested fields. We could see crops left behind, scraps punctuating the fields furrowed by the harvester's wheels. Then we came round a curve and there, just on the edge of the field, forlorn and all alone, sat an intact, single head of lettuce sitting *kerplunk* right on the edge of the field. I slowed and turned to look at Jim.

"Are you thinking what I'm thinking?" I asked.

"Absolutely," he replied as he dismounted his bike and walked down the slope. "Why not?" we squealed simultaneously.

"It'll be a great addition to dinner," Jim yelled as he picked it up, dusted it off and gently nestled it inside his pannier. The physical challenges of cycle touring aroused an enhanced awareness of sustenance. It's hard to explain the delight we both felt in coming across something as mundane as a head of lettuce, iceberg, no less. Lettuce, like bananas and eggs, didn't travel well. Lesson #13: Bad Things Can Happen to Good Food in Panniers. Bananas will always get mangled, eggs will always get broken. To find a pristine, free head of lettuce a couple of miles from the campground was delicious.

It was gloriously sunny as we remounted our bikes. "Who woulda thunk it?" I said, shaking my head. "Free lettuce for the taking."

"We're gonna have a great dinner tonight—too bad we only have one bottle of wine." Jim replied.

"Hardy-har," I laughed, "that'd sink us good. We've got two more days of cycling. Remember '*coupes les jambes*,' too much wine cuts the legs."

"A bottle-and-a-half then. Think this place might have a store?"

We made our way to the campground feeling giddy and strong. It had been an easy ride down the mountain, and then stumbled on the seemingly forgotten Santa Ynez River Valley, so pretty yet so depopulated. Traffic was light, even the one thousand-foot climb just before the campground didn't discourage us. And we got lucky. It turns out it's a challenge to secure a site at Jalama Beach. We arrived on a Sunday afternoon, just in time to grab a rare empty spot.

The campground was right on the beach, a glorified parking-lot-kinda place, four parallel, terraced levels, with hedges separating many, but not all sites. We once again were the odd guys out, just two bikes and a two-person tent. We attracted attention, even though they mercifully put us in a quiet back corner. We were right next to a solo guy with a lit-up Humvee. Joe was middle-aged, divorced, macho but no longer athletic. He used his vehicle to proclaim his manly prowess and search for babes. He invited us to share his campfire with that night's Babelicious—straight outa the fifties in capri pants and an exposed midriff top—but the fit seemed off enough we politely declined, and he didn't seem to mind.

We raced the sun to get dinner cooked before it set. There was no wind and temps were not quite as cold as the night before. Jim sautéed two chicken breasts in the lid of our three-piece cook set while I prepared the veggies. I shaped a plastic grocery bag into a bowl, added the gleaned lettuce, chopped veggies, sautéed chicken, and topped it with Jim's homemade dressing. Then I twisted it shut and shook it—voilà—tossed salad. Once the sun set and dinner was over, we had another reason to celebrate. On a whim, at the grocery store, I showed Jim a pack of fire starter sticks.

"Maybe we can have a mini-fire with these. Whaddya think?"

Jim looked at me like I was nuts, and then said, "Sure." So I bought them, a dozen sticks, each about an inch thick and six inches long.

We were usually the first to disappear for the night. There were several disadvantages to staying up late. First, we were pooped, second, we didn't have fancy equipment to make staying up late more pleasant—no table light to illuminate our site, no stash of firewood to warm us as the evening turned cold, no netting to protect us from the bugs. We fell asleep listening to the rest of the campers partying. Usually, I dropped off first, but sometimes Jim did if I was really engrossed in the maps.

But tonight, we had sticks, laughable, but what the hey? Some campgrounds sold a bag of logs, but we were still without paper, lighter fuel, or kindling. It was too much of a struggle to get logs started without those items, especially with how tired we found ourselves after a day of cycling. This early in our Great Experiment we considered it an achievement if we got all the dishes cleaned and gear put away before we climbed into the tent.

This campground was lively, neighborly. Many of the campers were regulars who knew each other. As darkness set in, there was a steady, happy hum, a buzz we could hear, the crinkling sound of campfires getting started, so this night, I giggled as we lit our sticks. I left it to Jim to get them started; I've little interest in fire starting, happily deferring the chore. It didn't take much, those sticks were loaded with lighter fluid. The only problem was there were only twelve sticks. Jim crunched up some pages from a free, local rag, built a teepee around them, and fired it up. Mini flames licked the sky, *mini* flames that is. I reached my hands out to enjoy the fleeting warmth. In less than ten minutes, it was dying down so Jim added the second stack and we got another ten minutes. "Too bad we didn't glean some logs," I joked.

"Let's walk the beach," Jim suggested as the last embers turned black. "There's a little bit of a moon." It was a lovely idea after a great day. We weren't the only ones who thought of it, but we had enough privacy in the semi-dark and it kept us out of the tent an extra hour.

After four days of cycling, it was sweet to pedal back to Buellton, take a nice hot shower, and sink into the big, soft, warm bed in our weatherproof motel room. Bookending our trip with a hotel room was luxurious. We got a great night's sleep and were up bright and early to get home in time to bake two pies for Thanksgiving dinner.

Santa Barbara Astronomical Unit telescope setup

Jim "harvesting" lettuce

NINE

Rock On

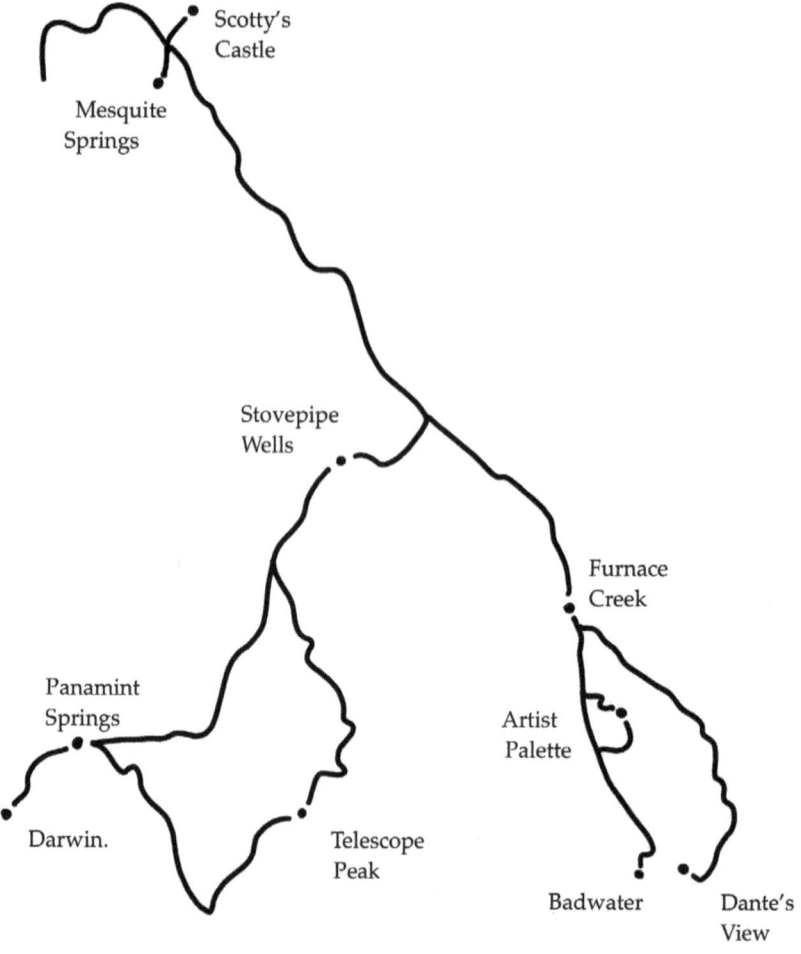

The life of the desert lives only by virtue of adapting itself to the conditions of the desert. Nature does not bend the elements to favor the plants and animals; she makes the plants and animals do the bending. —John C. Van Dyke

On the drive home from Buellton, we could barely stop talking about our latest Great Discovery. Although Jim was born and raised in California and I'd been here since age eighteen, we were experiencing a California we never knew. Some of these places we had been to before, some not, but we experienced it differently, at such a slow pace, we paid more attention. This state is BIG— 250 miles wide and 770 miles long—with incredible diversity of flora, fauna and landscape, but we found ourselves marveling over itty bitty places and minuscule details. In four days of cycling in Santa Barbara County, we traversed a swath about sixty miles, east to west, and yet were never bored. Like Jane Austen contentedly working on her two inches of ivory, we thrilled in the details we found in small spaces.

"Where next?" Jim asked after we exhausted recounting the trip's highlights. Looking at the calendar, I said "Spring semester doesn't start until the Tuesday after MLK Day; that's three weeks starting the day after Christmas. Got any ideas?"

"There's a place I've been wanting to go to for a while," Jim said. "Death Valley, I've got a great book that covers its geology. I'd love to check it out." I thought he was out of his mind. "Are you crazy? It's hot beyond belief, we'd roast to death riding in that heat, plus there's nothing there."

"It's not hot in winter." And so Jim began working on me, disabusing me of my ignorance. But I continued to resist, skeptical that a place with such a macabre name and reputation would be fun. He had a month to wear me down, but kicking and screaming, wear me down he did.

We assumed there was no way the national park would let us leave our car unattended for nine days, but I found a campground just outside the west side of the park, Panamint Springs. Not a hot springs, but a family-run motel/campground complex that had a store and a restaurant. Two outa three ain't bad. I called them and made the pitch: camp two nights, park our car for eight? Again, a pause and a shrug, and an *Okay, for an extra fee.*

The drive was much longer than our Northern California tours. Having driven it many times, I mostly ignored the first stretch, over Altamont Pass and down Highway 5 in San Joaquin Valley; but at the Tehachapis, I sat up and took notice. The landscape was so different from Nor Cal—the scrub-brush high dessert, forlorn, windswept towns hanging on for dear life. We didn't get to Panamint Springs until almost 4 p.m. and had to hustle to set up our tent before dark, but it was a nice place. The campsites were on the north side of the two-lane highway, a flattish, sandy spot with a semi-secluded, tent-only loop, separated by spindly willow trees. Lesson #14: All Campgrounds Are Not Alike. Our first trip camping among the trial bikers was a pleasant surprise. Since then, we increasingly found it not so much fun to pitch our tent in a sea of Whales with their exhaust, noisy generators. To find a campground that had a tent-only section was a treat. And this place had a restaurant so we didn't have to cook on the one-burner stove in the dark that night.

Chapter 9

We crossed the empty highway to a bare-bones restaurant with a futuristic flair—white plastic tables and chairs straight outa *The Jetsons*. Round, curvy, and pliable, the chairs even rotated. Jim squirmed and rolled his eyes as I acted like a six-year-old, spinning and spinning around. When the waitress, a perky brunette, arrived to take our order, she immediately responded, "Enjoying your ride?"

"Oh, yes. These chairs are great, I wish I could take them home with me," I joked.

"Well, you want all of them? You can have them." My eyes widened as I spun. "Turns out, the new boss hates them as much as you like them, and the minute he finds a buyer, they are outa here."

I looked around the room, four tables with four chairs each. "Oh, what am I gonna do with sixteen chairs?" I ask her, "How about two?"

She snorted as she flipped her pad to take our order, "Don't think so, darlin', it's all or nothing."

Traffic was nonexistent the next morning, the air brisk as we set off. The view was so vast, I felt so tiny. It was eight miles across this Panamint Valley, and then we had to climb up and over the Panamint Range, looming large in front of us, to get to Death Valley. Frankly, the massiveness of everything around me scared me—as we crossed the desolate valley, I wondered if we, 'er I, bit off more than I could chew.

It's hard to explain how demanding traveling only by the power of your body can be on your brain. The pacing, the grade, the wind, the distance, the weather—all are unknowns that can take us to our knees in seconds. We start out strong and eager, but most days, something tests us, sometimes a little, sometimes a lot, and sometimes too much. It's just us and the pedals against the elements.

We coined a phrase, *bonking*, for when one of us lost it; when the day turned so hard we just wanted to stop, give up then and there, not move another inch. I worried today might be one of those days for me. Everything was so big, so sparse. By now, cycle touring was the dominant focus of our free time. We loved it and couldn't wait for the next trip, but always each day had a degree of uncertainty.

Luckily, the climb was a gentle if long ascent, fourteen miles took two-and-a-half hours, a stunning pace of 5.6 mph. Relieved, we stopped at the Towne Pass elevation marker (4956 feet) for a photo and a hot soup break. And then, the payoff—a seventeen-mile, five thousand-foot drop with a view across the valley that went on forever, dusty, dry and rocky, as far as our eyes could see. I know I told you that the best downie we ever rode was down the south flank of Mount Lassen, but I lied. That was a mere three thousand-foot drop over six miles; today, we flew down 5,000 feet in sixteen miles, *flew*. And we could see miles and miles and miles of this vast valley, to the north and west—a shrubby rock fest.

We coasted into Stovepipe Wells campground, a dusty parking lot of a place with aluminum tables and one smelly restroom. The kind of campground one only stays in out of desperation. The next campground, Mesquite Spring, was another forty-two miles, and there was not enough vegetation anywhere to hide in, so we made the best of it, again climbing in the tent just after dark. We found two surprises in the morning, because we lazily went in the tent without properly cleaning up. The water in our mugs had turned to ice. And unexpected company left prints in the sand and my cap was gone. We looked everywhere, but Jim was convinced some four-legged critter made off with it. "Maybe

Chapter 9

not to eat," he said, "maybe to shred, to make a nest?" We'll never know, but we're pretty sure somewhere in that valley some critter has repurposed my cap.

We took off with the temps in the forties, traversing one of the defining features of the valley: long, slow, gradual ascents followed by brisk, easy-peasy descents. How do I explain this? The valley is framed by mountain ranges in every direction, and though it is a dry, virtually rainless place, that's not true in the mountains. If it snows or rains up in the mountains, it's gotta come down. Precipitation in the mountains has to come down. It picks up speed on the comparatively vegetation-less slopes, faster and faster, carrying rocks and debris, then slowing down as the slope decreases, eventually rolling to a stop in the flat valley, depositing whatever came with it. Multiply that by thousands of times over millions of years. The debris fanned out, and the mouth of every canyon in the valley now has a gradual, cone-shaped slope that rolls down and meets the valley like a rounded fan. As a result, the valley is anything but flat—it's a vast, undulating landscape; the main roads are gentle roller coaster ribbons of asphalt through a shrubby, rocky landscape. Our first day was one long, slow uppie, and one fast descent to enter the valley. Today, was a series of roly-polies—slow, fairly easy climbs and brisk downies as we headed north to Mesquite Springs.

"Look," Jim shouted, "Stop!" I turned to see a vast, golden-sable sand dune about 200 feet high rising out of the scrub to our left. We could see little dots of people climbing as the morning sun lit up the dunes and cast dramatic shadows.

Along the road, scrubby, hardy little plants kept us company, desperate little numbers with tiny yellow and purple petals, scratchy leaves, eking out an existence in this middle of nowhere and nothing, sparking our admiration. They appeared often enough to inspire us with their pluckiness as we went up and down the slopes. Why, if they could thrive here, we could, too.

The landscape was mesmerizing, the valley enormous, ringed in by vast mountain ranges scraping the blue sky with its jagged profile as far as the eye can see. Arid, scrappy brush, dust, and, oh—the colors—pastel grays, beiges, browns, sun-bleached greens, and a vast, most often cloudless blue sky. The distant grays played tricks on my eyes, turning into purples, the sands became yellows, the brown bushes turned orange, the dessert was a light show of pastels. Dirt and dust, sand and rocks, scrappy bushes, over and over again, following the asphalt up the gentle alluvial slopes and sliding down the other side, for the forty-two miles it took us to get to the campground. By the time we arrived at Mesquite, I was in love. Who woulda thunk it?

Mesquite Springs was an empty, isolated campground at the northern end of the valley's asphalt road, an odd place in the middle of nowhere. But like all human settlements in Death Valley, it's there for one reason: water. All developments in the valley are where they are because there's a natural water source nearby. There was thirty campsites but only three campers that night. Scotty's Castle was less than ten miles from the campground, but the area was so desolate (even by Death Valley standards), most campers drove up from Furnace Creek for the day.

Leaving our gear in the tent, next morning we took off unloaded early to tour Scotty's Castle, a curious blend of opulent detail and ragged decay. Acquired by the national park in 1970, the castle and its furnishings were stunning but the outer buildings and grounds were pretty rough. Oh, it killed me to tour the unfinished, dilapidated swimming pool. The current preference with those in the historic-preservation business is to preserve a site in the style of its time. That meant the unfinished pool would stay unfinished. I mean, talk about unclear on the concept. They've got a stunning, big, unfinished pool in the middle of this hot-house furnace, and they chose not to finish it? Just because the 1929 Stock Market Crash left Chicago millionaire Albert Johnson short of cash? Sadists, they are. Even on this sixty-five-degree day in January, I woulda jumped in, but the purists want to be "historically accurate."

Next morning, we headed south to Furnace Creek, the beating heart of this massive, notorious national park, a spring-fed oasis that had everything that the rest of the valley didn't: multiple campgrounds, restaurants, swimming pool, a history museum, visitors center, even a luxury hotel with spa, and—just ridiculous in this water-forsaken landscape—a golf course, all thanks to an ever-bubbling supply of spring water. We made our way to the far back of the main campground, to the walk-in-only/tent-only campsites.

We set up the tent and took off on unloaded bikes. Lesson #15: Cycling on a Bike with no Panniers is Heavenly. It's the best thing to do, second only to taking a full day of rest, to take a spin *sans* baggage. It's delicious how light and feathery an unloaded bike feels, especially after days of loaded riding. The next three days, we camped in the Death Valley version of the lap of luxury, with our tent within walking distance of food, dining, swimming, and entertainment (the ranger's nightly programs—I mean, what does that say about a place that the evening highlight is the ranger program?), and spent several days cycling to several of the valley's more famous sites, all within a day's ride of Furnace Creek.

Jim was keen to bike to Badwater, as much for the geology as the topography. Just twenty miles south, a gentle ride to the pancaked landscape that is Badwater the lowest point in Death Valley (and North America)—282 feet below sea level. We pulled up to an odd site, part moonscape, part tourist mecca. There were several buses unloading dozens of tourists hitting as many Death Valley highlights as they could squeeze into a one-day drive over from their hotels in Las Vegas.

A bonus awaited us on the return: Artist's Palette, one of the most popular sites in the valley. If I had been struck by the colors each day so far, here was a revelation: the dusky pastel palette of sun-bleached rocks gave way to a riot of pinks and burnt sierras, greens and ochers. The explosion of colors convinced Jim to do something he almost would never do—leave our locked bikes unattended to hike to the colors up close. Anxious about the bikes, we set off at a fast enough clip that we soon came upon and passed a family of four. As we surveyed the colors, we heard the mother say, "Even with biking up that road, they walked up this hill faster than us." Jim and I looked at each other, smiled, and realized she was right. We were in such good shape the climb didn't seem much. And the ride back was a skinny roller coaster ribbon lacing through narrow canyons—no wonder the road was one way. Back at the campground, we made a beeline for the pool; the campground didn't have showers, but the pool did.

After five days of cycling, we were feeling pretty buff and decided to bite off a piece we weren't sure we could chew— Dante's View was twenty-six miles from our campground

Chapter 9

and 5,500 feet higher. Oh, this ride was different in a way we didn't expect. The roly-poly landscape up and down the alluvial fans gave a pleasant pacing to each day's ride: slow uppies for a while, brisk downies, repeat, repeat, repeat. The ride to Dante's View was an unrelenting, steady uppie with the final quarter mile too steep for me. I had to walk as all the tourists watched (oh, the shame). Not Jim—he pedaled his way up. We were thrilled to get off the bikes and take a break, but it so was windy and cold that we soaked in the view and headed back down. It took us five hours and twenty minutes to get to the top, and only sixty-five minutes to get back.

We recovered enough on the downie that when we got to the turnoff for Zabriskie Point, just six miles before Furnace Creek, we turned to check it out. Two-tenths of a mile in, where the paved parking lot ended and a path began, we read the sign: pedestrians only beyond this point. Jim looked at me, "You thinking what I'm thinking?" I looked over my shoulder back at the mostly empty parking lot, looked up the mostly empty path.

"If you're thinking let's bike up the path, then, yeah." Jim smiled as I put my foot back on the pedal. He knows how much I love to break rules. We did encounter a few people coming down the path as we biked up, but we gave them wide berth. There were a fair number of people at the top, it was a short distance, but they ignored us as we ignored them. It was easy to do—the scenery was so stunning, quiet, desolate, vast. Deep ridges in earthy pastel colors ran the gamut, though colors not as varied or bright as at Artist's Palette. Again, we headed straight for the pool and went back to the tent to put on our sparkling best for dinner at the steakhouse saloon. Ah, the high life. It's a bit embarrassing to admit how large food looms in our imagination. I was about two steps ahead of Jim the entire half-mile walk from the campground. We entered a dark wood Western-themed affair. We sat in a booth; I love a soft, cocoon-y booth as much as I love a loop, especially after a long ride. Steaks and fries, washed down with wine, and Jim even got pie à la mode for desert and let me have a bite. No bare-bones campground dinner tonight, we went to bed content.

When it was time to return to the car we left the valley the long way, climbing to the remote Wildrose Campground at 4100 feet. It was so cold we headed for our tent after eating an early dinner. Lesson #16: Traveling by Bicycle Cancels Campfires. It's not possible to carry firewood, and more often than not, there's never enough nearby salvageable firewood, especially in a treeless desert like Death Valley. Long ago, we accepted that the ritual of an evening toasty campfire would rarely be part of our travels. But this night, a carrot-top young man in dusty clothes approached just as we were about to call it a night. "Hi," he said. "We're about to start a fire, looks unlikely you'll be having one. Would you like to join us?"

"Sure," we said simultaneously as we looked at each other, "we'd love it."

"I'm Aiden," he said as he turned to go. "Strick is just getting the fire started. Come on over whenever you're ready." As much as we loved to complain about RVs, we were both shameless enough to accept an invitation to enjoy the amenities they afforded when the opportunity arose.

Strick, tall, with jet-black hair, was working on the fire as we approached and made introductions.

"I'm sorry," I said. "This is our last night on the road and our larder is really low, all we have to share is a bag of Fritos."

"Fritos," Strick said, "I love Fritos, and they go great with beer. Would you like a Sierra Nevada?" Aiden heard us and arrived with four beers and a bowl for the Fritos. The fire was terrific. We brought over our legless chairs, and when we propped them on boulders, the two guys laughed.

"Desperate times call for desperate measures," I said. It was a nice evening, Strick and Aiden were architecture majors at Cal Poly, both in their senior year.

"We wanted to check out the Charcoal Kilns for our senior project. Then, we hiked to Telescope Peak, 11,000 feet." Strick said. Jim peppered them with questions. He would have loved to have had the time to hike there, but I knew that would have to wait until a car-camping trip, so I just listened while the three of them went on and on.

Gazing out the window as our car slowly chugged up the Tehachapi Summit, I exclaimed. "Amazing, what a trip, I much prefer desert to jungle. And Van Dyke was right."

"We'll have to come back," Jim replied. "They say March is the best month for wildflowers, and it's not as cold as January." The immovable landscape bent us to its will, but we felt like rosy-cheeked kids coming in from the snow. I could hardly believe that I had fallen in love with Death Valley. We couldn't wait to come back again. When?

Rocking into Death Valley

Jim at Badwater

Climbing to Artist Palette

View of Death Valley from Dante's Peak

TEN

Anne Gets Her First Ten-Speed

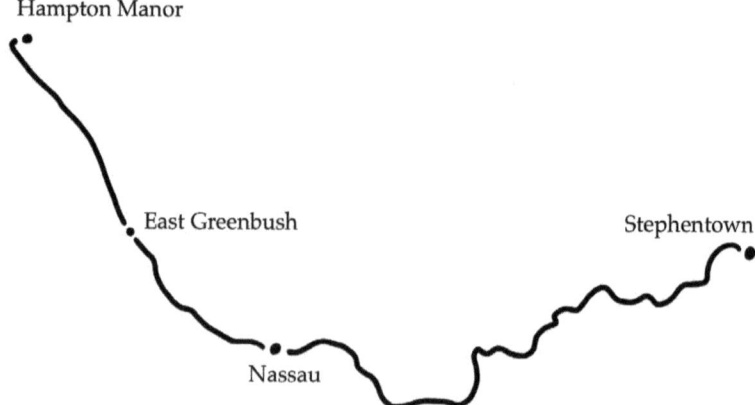

Among a certain set of teenagers, ten-speed bikes were all the rage for Christmas my junior year in high school. That spring, after the snow melted, those of us with our new toys (but still too young to afford cars) started connecting via bicycle, liberating ourselves from riding buses or begging rides. The rolling hills of our Hudson River Valley community were a pain, but once we mastered shifting the ten-speeds, our young bodies were soon able handle most of the climbs.

My best friend at the time, Mary, also got a bike. It was an unusual gift as neither of us came from families flush with cash. The bikes were big, sparkly, and looked expensive. Maybe it was a measure of how desperate our parents were to figure out the perfect Christmas gift for teenage girls.

In grade school, Mary and I grew up blocks from each other in Hampton Manor, a compact neighborhood with many Catholic families whose lives were centered around the church and its elementary school. Later, in public high school, we reconnected as kindred spirits/survivors finally freed of the Mercy nuns, as we tried to make our way and fit into a school with kids who had a lot more than we did.

By junior year, we were thick as thieves; we went everywhere and did everything together. Our new bikes reinforced the bond. We were both middle daughters, though she was the middle child of three girls while I had five older and four younger siblings. We both had brown hair; mine was curlier, though Mary's was a much prettier deep redbrown. We both had freckles, but she had way more than I.

It turned out that several of the more avid new riders shared the same English teacher, Mr. McCann. When he learned that some of his students were cycling around Rensselaer County, he invited those who were strong enough to make the trip to his Stephentown home—in the foothills of the Taconic Mountains and the southeast corner of the county. A core group became a kind of a club, centered around cycling and with an affinity for their teacher, a first-generation Irish immigrant with a strong accent and relaxed demeanor.

When Mary and I overheard some students talking in the cafeteria about their most recent ride, we asked if we could tag along on the next one. The thing was, most of the kids in the cycling group lived more toward the eastern end of the school district, whereas Mary and I lived at the western edge. Once we committed to joining them, we had to get to the group's starting point, eleven miles east. We were unable to find anyone with a pickup to carry us and our ten-speeds, so we hopped on our bikes that Saturday morning.

This was pre-freeway sixties. Governor Rockefeller had not yet defaced the Capitol District with imitation-California freeway monstrosities, so there was a lot of traffic on Columbia Turnpike. By the time the traffic slowed at Schodack Center when Routes 9 and 20 split, Mary and I were windblown and disheveled.

We pressed on, young and keen to have fun on our new wheels. We really needed a break by the time we met up with the group in Nassau. They told us we were sixteen miles from Stephentown. Mary and I looked at each other but said nothing, trying to hide how worn out we already were.

We were a motley crew that mild spring day. No helmets, no special biking clothes or gear. I don't think any of us even had water bottles. Prim and proper, Jean was the heart of the group. She had McCann as her teacher and was involved in several school clubs (theater, journalism) that he advised. Andy was a slight, earnest young man with a playful twinkle in his eyes (who would go on to become a preacher). Jimmy had dirty blond curly hair and an infectious sense of humor, always telling jokes. Steve seemed a sensitive soul, hanging back and watching through his very dark brown eyes. Dian and Jeanne were first cousins who lived a few blocks from each other. Dian was a tiny brunette with big, almond eyes. Like me, she had a lot of brothers, but she lost her mother a few years earlier. Jeanne was a goofy, happy blond, and along with a brother, adopted and spoiled by a couple desperate to be parents. Mary and I soon became enamored with the two very different cousins, and before long, we were an inseparable foursome.

We all followed Jean's lead, continuing on Route 20 east, with little traffic through bucolic rolling green hills. I'm sure the vehicles found us an unusual sight in this backwater corner of the county. Besides the farms, the big deals out here were the Lebanon Valley Speedway and Shaker Village. We missed both of them by turning off Route 20 for the even pokier, skinnier, and hillier Route 26 that took us to Stephentown. There was pretty much nothing but green here, except for the hamlet of East Nassau, where we stopped at a mom-and-pop shop for cold drinks. Forests and farmland kept us company on the uphill climb, distracting us all from the pain.

We were all pretty sweaty upon arrival and happy to get off our bikes. The kids who cycled only from Nassau immediately started goofing around in the yard, but Mary and I just sat on the grass, too tired to move. Our first big ride— we were breaking in our bikes, or were they breaking us in? We'd ridden twenty-seven miles, ouch, and we had to retrace them to get home. I did my best to hide the shock.

"Congratulations," Mr. McCann exclaimed as he came out his front door with two big pitchers, one of lemonade and one of ice water, "We're at 1,100 feet here, more or less, while the high school is only 300 feet." *And Hampton Manor is even lower,* I thought. Mr. McCann lived in a charming stone house with a sprawling, sloped lawn, not far from the Massachusetts border.

"Quite a climb," said his wife, Karen, following him with a huge tray of sandwiches. "Help yourselves. You all must be very hungry and thirsty." She served sandwiches and lemonade outside on shaded, rustic wood tables. Their baby boy, less than a year old, slept in a sun-dappled stroller just outside the back door. I kept to the background; though Mr. McCann was warm and welcoming, I didn't have him as a teacher. We stayed only a couple of hours, and those with excess energy played frisbee after eating. Mary and I both opted to doze in the grass. McCann looked the part of an Irish man of letters—in a saggy tweed jacket with hunched-over shoulders and thick brown hair like JFK's, combed with a part. Shorter than some students, barely a decade older, married and a new father, he made us all feel at ease.

It was still a long way back, so we bid the teacher and his young family goodbye and retraced our route, much quieter this time. The first stretch to Nassau was mostly a downhill, though there was a big climb before the village. Mary and I had another eleven miles to go and went slower with each mile. By the time we got home, we were barely peddling fast enough to stay upright. We didn't even say goodbye when we parted for the final blocks to our houses just as the sun set.

The fifty-four-mile day translated into two very sore bodies; the last few miles were especially grueling. Mary and I never made that ride again, since we knew how hard it really

CHAPTER 10

was. If someone with a pickup drove us to Nassau, we might have considered it. But we didn't. Mary pretty much had her fill of distance riding; the bloom was off the rose for her.

But I had a brand-new love, and it wasn't a boy. I stayed hooked on biking. I just loved the sheer physicality of riding, the freedom from cars and restrictions. It opened a window for me, a way to get away, to explore, be dependent on no one. I even placed an ad in *The Crossroads Gem*, my high-school newspaper: "Anyone interested in bicycling to California? If you are, talk to Anne Breedlove." I didn't get any takers. But I didn't forget. I left my first ten-speed behind when I moved out. I don't even remember what make and model it was, but one of the first things I acquired once I moved to San Francisco the next year was a bike. It would take almost forty years for me to find someone game enough to join me in realizing my cross-country dream.

My first classified in The Crossroads Gem

ELEVEN

Snow for Easter

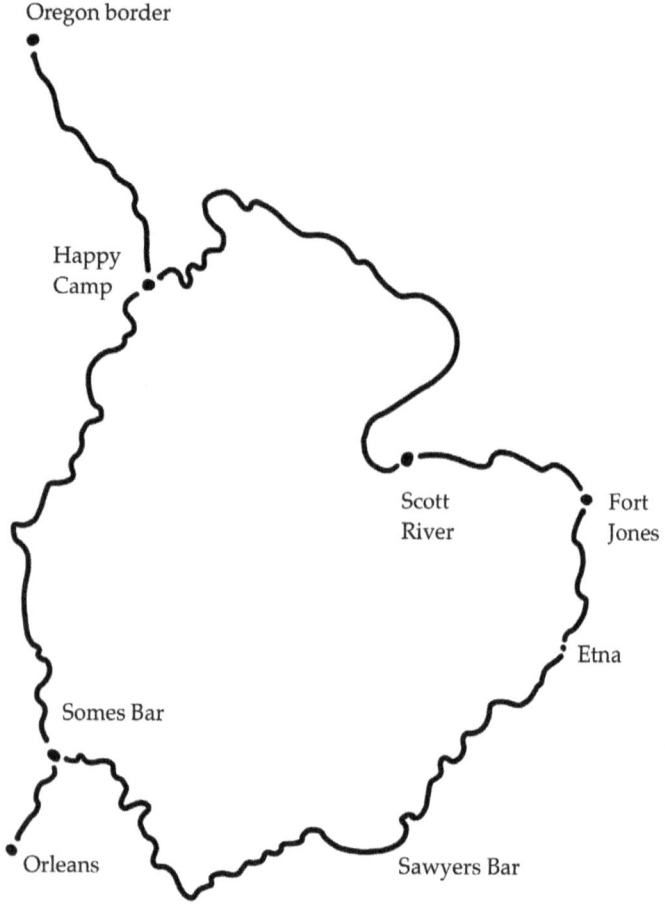

Death Valley was months behind as we prepped the garden for summer planting. As Jim huffed and puffed, lugging the rototiller out of the shed he said, "I want another new challenge. Where can we go that's new?" *Here we go again*, I thought as I laid out the seed packets and trays, *Mr. Spontaneity strikes again*, but I was ready for him this time.

"I get the second week of April for spring break this year, that's nine days. We could go back to Death Valley if April isn't too hot, but Easter in April means it might be warm enough to go north." I looked up as I was filling the trays with potting soil and continued, "I found another loop, up in Siskiyou County, two hundred miles, probably with less traffic in spring than in summer. This loop will be The Loop of Loops— following three rivers—the Scott, the Klamath, and the Salmon—for about 90 percent of the time. Is that new enough?" Jim bent over and pumped the gas line, he hadn't used it since last fall it was always hard to start after so long.

"Sounds good, but that far north in April? I'm not sure." He yanked the starter handle hard, one, two, three times. No go. "Shit, why is this thing always so hard to start. Okay, okay, leave me be, let's do it." He bent over and pulled the starter cord another four times until finally the engine came to life. Decision made and conversation over.

Four weeks and a six-hour drive up Highway 5 later we arrived in the tiny town of Fort Jones. We stopped in Redding to fuel up the car and eat at Black Bear Diner. The dramatic ascent around Mount Shasta revealed a lot of snow. After getting permission, we parked our car at Fort Jones

Ranger Station, loaded up the bikes, and pedaled fifteen mostly downhill miles to Indian Scotty campground. There was a closed sign on the big metal gate. Another first. Jim looked at me with a little bit of steam coming out of his ears—was it the cold or was he peeved? We had free-camped before, on the Lost Coast and Mount Lassen, but I assumed campgrounds would be open for spring break. I knew (but he didn't, yet), that there wasn't another campground for quite a while.

"Let's just go around the gate and camp—who'll even know we're here?" I blurted out.

"Whaddya crazy? It's not safe, we might get discovered, there's no water . . ." Jim took off his helmet and wiped the sweat off his forehead. He always gets sweat in his eyes, especially when he gets upset. Things weren't looking good.

Still working from the optimistic side of the equation, I replied, "Sure it's safe. The gate is locked; nobody—but us—is gonna come in. Cars can't get around the gate, but we can." I tried to keep my voice calm and confident. "Why, we'll have the whole campground to ourselves. No generators, no smokers, no dogs. And the Scott River is right there. We can pull cold water right out of it." Jim wasn't happy but I waited and let the idea sink in.

"Besides, what choice do we have?" I continued, delivering the final blow. "There isn't another campground for twenty miles, and who knows if that one is open?" I had him at twenty miles. No way we were gonna ride another twenty today.

And so, on our eighth bike adventure, we again discovered one of the truly greatest joys of cycle touring: free-camping, and it gave me so much pleasure. I'd put in my time—nine years of chaffing under the capricious and

Chapter 11

arbitrary dictates of Catholic nuns. As a result, I came away with several important skill sets: the multiplication tables, tidy handwriting (when I was younger), the ability to diagram a sentence, and, drum roll, leaping at any and all opportunities to do an end-run around authority.

After taking a few more minutes to accept the situation, Jim pushed his bike around the closed gate and I followed. We toured the whole place. Jim picked out a heavily wooded site in the way back, well hidden from either the entrance or the road. Then he took off to pull water out of the river and returned a changed man.

"I left the bottle of wine nestled under a rock in the river—we're going to have cold Sauv Blanc with dinner tonight. And I scouted out the road," he added. "I think we're hidden well enough that I'm going to collect dropped wood for a campfire. We're gonna live it up tonight."

After brewing some hot tea, I took out my legless chair and happily recounted the day's turn of events in my journal. While Jim started the fire, I started to prepare dinner—now-defrosted cod filets, couscous, salads, and a baguette (first night's camp dinner is always the best). I left the cod for the better chef to sauté. Jim hiked back down to the river, brought back the cold bottle of wine, and the party began. We didn't enter the tent until the campfire was thoroughly out and still we had enough wood left over. Jim said we'd have another fire in the morning. As we approached the closed gate to leave the next morning, Jim yelled "Stop!" He heard a truck on the road. We held back until it passed. Another pattern: it was very important to Jim to free-camp only where he believed no one could possibly find us, and not be seen heading into or out of the area. As eager as I was to get going, I stopped, humoring him now was worth it.

Who knows what challenges awaited us? We followed the Scott River through thick forest—oh, it was beautiful. The road is mostly downhill from Fort Jones to Happy Camp. The river was bursting, the sporadic sound of crashing water a lovely accompaniment to the click of our bikes. The hamlet of Scott Bar had a historical marker for John Scott, the first to discover gold in these parts in 1850. Erected in 1941 (by the Sons and Daughters of the Pioneers of Scott Bar) right across the street from the old schoolhouse (built 1890), it had two plaques embedded in a granite boulder surrounded by a quaint Victorian iron fence. Just past where the Scott flowed into the Klamath was another hamlet, Hamburg, with a campground and a general store. Next came Seiad Valley, with a gas station, general store, two RV parks, café, elementary school, and a tavern/lodge. Many of the businesses had signs offering their wares to Pacific Crest Trail hikers. The Wildwood Tavern & Lodge also had a sign: Since 1929, the official tavern of the State of Jefferson with a big round yellow circle with two black XXs in the middle. What was that about?

We stopped for lunch in the dreary town of Happy Camp (maybe it used to be, but it sure didn't feel happy to me), the only place, so far, that was big enough to qualify as a town as it had our Big Three: grocery, restaurant, and library, but the poverty was sobering. It was also the headquarters of the Karuk tribe and had an airstrip. Heading out of town, we found the library, and I went in to ask about the state of Jefferson, as we had seen numerous of the double X yellow signs all day. The young librarian gave me a brochure.

Back in 1941, quite a number of Northern Californians and Southern Oregonians were unhappy enough with how little attention they received from their state capitals that they made a national plea to form a new state, stopping traffic on Highway 99 and handing out "Proclamation of Independence" flyers. Alas, a week later, Pearl Harbor and the subsequent entry into World War II extinguished the effort, but the sentiments live on.

I wondered about the unborn state of Jefferson as we rode. The landscape tells a story, the history of a place. We saw lots of evidence of former mines and lumber mills, gone now, the jobs went with them. What's left? Great economic disparity abounds in rural Northern California; lots of ramshackle buildings, some toppling over, far fewer well-kept establishments. I wondered how much the nostalgia for a new state is fueled by economic impoverishment?

Our destination for that night, West Branch Campground, was on the State of Jefferson Scenic Byway, so before leaving town, we picked up some groceries and then rode north out of town along Indian Creek. On an isolated but open stretch of road, we encountered seven deer. Three crossed the road in front of us, but four stood stock still until we got right up to them. They started to run parallel to us as they tried to get across; three of them finally cutting in front of me—only ten feet ahead. Then they leapt into the field on our left and were gone. We were struck by how close they got to us, we were both worried we might collide. Another first, cycling with deer. We already had experience with cycling with sheep and cows, startled, but running along the fences that separated us.

After a few more miles, we again arrived at a campground with a padlocked gate and a sign saying it opened for the season in two days. In we went, it was great to "free" camp with a picnic table.

We woke next morning, Easter Sunday, to bright sunshine.

"Jim," I said, "the map says we're only nine miles south of the Oregon border, and our next campground is only thirty-four miles south. Want to try to get to Oregon, just for the hell of it?" I laughed tentatively as I added, "It's probably 3,000 feet higher, though."

"That'll be eighteen extra miles? Added to thirty-four, equals fifty-two. We can do that. I'm game if you are."

After an hour, drifts of snow started piling up in the shady spots. After two hours, banks of snow on the side of the road were obviously thrown up by snowplows. Then the two-lane road narrowed to one lane fenced in by three-foot-high banks of snow. And at three hours, we had to stop since we faced a white wall. The road was surrounded by snow banks four feet high. In a clearing on the side of the road sat two idle snow plows. We looked over the snowbank and could see a mirror image about two hundred yards away, two more snow plows parked. We were close enough to see Oregon, but we would not be reaching the border today, not without snow shoes. Obviously, the two crews meet at the border. It was likely they'd finish the clearing the next day, Monday.

We had the snowy world to ourselves, so we sat on the sun-warmed asphalt and pulled out the thermos of hot soup, surrounded by white. It smelled different, and the view was terrific. We were at 4,800 feet and picnicked on the sun-warmed asphalt in a sea of glistening white.

We turned around to retrace our path and again saw four deer who ran with us along the side of the road. Two cut right in front of us and crossed to the other side, leaping over a six-foot-high fence, clearing it by two feet, easy.

Chapter 11

It was still before noon, so we blazed through a not-yet-awake Happy Camp, another pattern discovered: Sunday mornings are the quietest time of the week, therefore, the best time for carefree cycling. Beyond Happy Camp, we reconnected with the stupendous Klamath and soon passed a number of rafting outfitters. One establishment forced us to stop in our tracks—a wood-beamed ranch house with wrap-around porch and formidable notched-log fence with that bright reddish-orange of new wood—but everything—house, porch, fence, trees, yard, was covered in white. It was a winter wonderland of ice and icicles because the sprinkler system was going full blast. Yet, the sprinkler water reached up six feet so the bottom half of the bushes and trees were covered in ice but anything higher was bare branches. Such an incongruous sight. Not too much further, at fifty-four miles for the day, we stopped at yet another closed-until- tomorrow forest service campground, Dillon Creek. We were too close to the road to dare a campfire, but for a third night, we had the place to ourselves.

At the confluence of the Klamath and Salmon Rivers the next day, we bid adieu to cycling downstream to follow the Salmon up and over the mountains. It was hot, and for a long stretch, we had the full sun on us.

"Stop!" Jim yelled as we pass a small creek flowing down the cliff to the river below. With that, he ripped off his shirt, dunked it in the cold water, and put it back on. "Do it, too," he insisted, "it'll cool us off in this heat." And so Jim invented Lesson #17: If It's Hot and There's Cold Water, Jump In. That afternoon, the Monday after Easter, we pulled into an open campground. As it had been almost four days since we showered and the cold water felt so good on the way up, it didn't take too much to convince Jim to take a dip in the River.

Now, usually I'm the speed demon—my strategy with cold water is just bite the bullet, full-body immersion, last as many seconds—maybe minutes—as I can depending on the temp, and get out. Jim, on the other hand, is a sensitive soul and prefers to dip in by inches. But he surprised me, and as I turned around after dropping my clothes on the rocks, he shouted, "I'm so stinking I'm just going all in." And then he did, head first. I watched his toes disappear in the water and then *BOOM!* The top half of his body shot straight up like a rocket. "Owww!" gasping in shock, he scrambled out before I even got my feet wet. I stifled a laugh as I waded ankle deep and debated how much further I wanted to go in. How bad did I smell, really?

No sooner had we started cooking dinner that it started to rain. A ranger stopped by and warned us a big one was rolling in that night and would likely take a day or two to pass. We raced to finish dinner and clean up, and when we finally piled into the tent, it was pouring.

"I hope there isn't too much rain and that the equipment holds up," Jim said. But it wasn't long before we noticed that moisture was condensing all around the base of the tent. Jim went out to check things before it got good and dark and came back concerned.

"We staked the tent in a culvert. And," he said, "this tent isn't waterproof."

"Oh no!" I exclaimed as I headed out of the tent and looked around. The entire base of the tent was already soaked. We were the only campers, so genius that I am, I said, "Let's move the tent into the restroom vestibule. "It can fit under the overhang and will protect us."

"I don't know," he replied, "What if other campers show up?" But things were looking grim. There wasn't anybody else here, yet there were two restrooms at opposite ends of the small campground. We were at the far end, the vestibule was covered, and the tent fit. So we each picked up two corners and moved it, climbed back in, and began a night of fitful sleep. About midnight, we were awakened by a camper van pulling in. Jim was not happy with my idea, and within twenty minutes, some guy showed up to use the pit toilet. Jim went out to apologize and came back in to insist we move the tent again. Once I'm in bed for the night, that's it.

"No way," I refused. "Guys don't need toilets. How many ever really walk all the way to a toilet when they can do it outside? I'm not moving. If they gotta go number two, they can use the toilet at the other end."

"Why did I let you convince me to do this?" he asked, exasperated, "How am I gonna sleep now, worrying about the leaks and those guys?" We did not have one of our better nights.

It wasn't raining when we woke, just dripping. Mortified by the failure of his equipment (and that other men knew he had equipment failure), Jim put us on the fast track. We ate cold bagels washed down with cold, instant coffee, yuck—my standards are much lower than Jim's, I needed the caffeine, and left at 8:25 a.m. to the smells of bacon and pancakes at the guys' campsite. By the time we got to the road, it was gloriously sunny with that glistening, after-the-rain look. The trees were steaming as we biked up another sensational gorge. Truly breathtaking.

The Klamath and Salmon Rivers are a wonder. In some places, we were atop a sheer cliff, hundreds of feet above the water, then we'd dip down to the water and up again. And the wildflowers were blooming. Little white ones, yellow ones that looked related to orchids, purple ones as well, and blue and pink. I didn't know the names of any of them, but enjoyed their company.

In the hamlet of Forks of Salmon, we stopped at what passed for a general store, a shabby-chic trailer. I chatted briefly with the owner as she rang up our purchases. She told me she sells mostly junk food out of the trailer. Her late nineteenth-century building burned down in '92 and the county won't let her rebuild because the original wood building was built on dirt, no foundation. Because there was no remaining footprint, they put the kibosh on the rebuild. No wonder there are so many yellow and black double X signs. Then we bought some fresh fruit and veggies from a guy parked out front who drives around all the remote areas delivering them, like my parents had eggs, milk, and bread delivered in the '50s.

When we set up camp for our final night, at an open but mostly empty Idlewild Campground, almost everything we had was damp. Not only was our tent truly not waterproof, neither were our panniers. Equipment Guy Jim was mortified that his equipment didn't pass muster.

"We're going to have to get a new tent," Jim said as we cooked dinner and the rain started yet again, "and new waterproof panniers, too." I knew he was right, no way did we want a repeat of this soggy mess. We went to bed early since we had a long climb in the morning, 4,000 feet in ten miles. I didn't sleep well. Besides being damp, I worried whether I would be able to handle the next day.

When Jim woke me at 6:15, it was raining, so we ate another cold breakfast in the tent, raced to pack and broke camp by 7:40. At least our rain jackets and pants were waterproof. The first five miles weren't too hard, though it rained continually. Then the slope got steep enough that I struggled to stay upright. Around this time, the rain turned to gently falling snow. The good news was the road builders put in a lot of switchbacks, and a switchback typically flattens out a bit on the curves. That's where I would stop when I had to rest. Once I stop, though, I worry about remounting without falling over. And that anxiety gets into my head, start/stop, start/stop. Then, with several miles to the top, everything was white. It built up fast and thick in the woods, but melted on the road, we followed the black ribbon through the whiteness. We slowly climbed with snow falling so thickly we had zero visibility, barely able to see each other six feet apart. It was quiet, still. Magical. The challenge of the climb forgotten by the beauty.

It took us three-and-a-quarter hours more to summit. At the peak, we stopped long enough to add a layer of fleece for the ride down, barely speaking so as not to pierce the stillness. All the way up, I looked forward to finishing the climb and enjoying the downie, but a mile or so down, the snow turned back into rain and the grade was steep enough we had to ride our brakes—it was too dangerous to go fast with the rain and ice. We didn't have waterproof gloves so our hands froze, meaning they didn't grab so well and worked more like claws, but we had to keep squeezing. Finally, my hands hurt so bad, I stopped and collapsed into tears on the side of the road.

As I sobbed, Jim took off my gloves and buried my frozen hands in his armpits under his jacket and squeezed as he said, "Why didn't we buy those mini heat packs at REI? That's exactly what we need right now." We sat down on a boulder under a big tree that sheltered us a bit and he took out the thermos full of hot soup. We sipped it as we warmed our hands around our mugs. Jim noticed three large, blue eggs in full sunlight nestled on leaves at the base of a big rock. They were about four inches long. No mother or nest or cover to protect them. Not up in a tree, not in a nest. If the eggs could survive this harsh climate, surely we could, too. The hot soup revived us enough to buck it up for the remaining fifteen miles to the car, and it got easier the more we descended as the temperature rose and the rain lessened.

It felt so good to finally get off the saddles at the car. We just threw everything in, soaking wet. Jim put the heater on full blast and announced, "You realize we can't stop at Harbin on the way home, everything is too wet to set up for another night, especially if it's raining there, which is likely. I think it's best if we just head straight home."

I didn't say no. Being inside the car, warm and dry after days of rain and cold and snow, it was easy for me to let go of soaking in Harbin—this time. I drifted off to sleep as Jim waxed rhapsodic about the new equipment he planned to buy.

This trip hit so many buttons for us, even with the soggy weather and soggier gear. It was a loop, and except for the climb on the last day, up and over the six thousand-foot Mount Etna, we pedaled 220 miles along three stunning rivers. The traffic was minimal; Siskiyou County was as isolated as the Lost Coast, which meant we could better enjoy the spectacular views, tight ravines, steep cliffs, forested mountains, and crashing water. Again, unexpected discoveries. Closed campgrounds, dramatic gorges, snow and ice, tawdry towns and hamlets—once again, cycling left us eager for more.

Stopped by snow a quarter mile short of the Oregon border

View of the Klamath River

Climbing west side Mt. Etna

Taking a needed break along the Salmon River

TWELVE

We B Animals

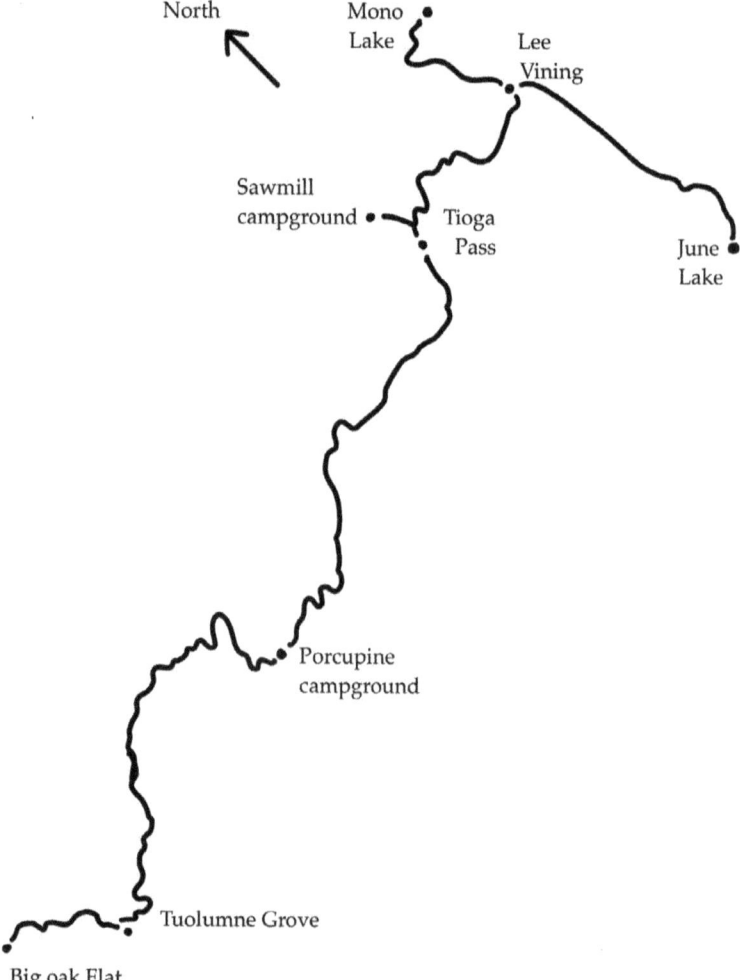

With my summer semester over at the end of July, Mr. Spontaneity was again itching for somewhere new.

"How about Yosemite?" he suggested as he worked on the bikes in the garage.

"But the valley is a zoo in the summer," I objected.

"What about the northern part? Tioga Pass Road runs a long east–west path; what if we tried that?" He said as he replaced the tires on our bikes. "We can christen these new Schwalbe tires." So I got out our old Yosemite maps and studied them. It was about a hundred miles from the Big Oak Flat entrance on Highway 120 all the way to Mono Lake on 395 in the parched, eastern Sierra dessert. And oodles of camping opportunities, legitimate and otherwise, along the way.

A week after I finished grading, we made the five-hour drive across the Sacramento Valley and up the Sierra foothills to the entrance to Yosemite on Highway 120, Big Oak Flat. Again, the Designated-by-Jim Representative (me) walked into the visitor's center, a funky dilapidated wooden building with tourists searching for the perfect souvenir and backpackers studying maps for the best routes. I spilled our plans to the ranger at the counter.

"Could we leave our car in some far corner of the lot for two nights?" To say he was skeptical was an understatement.

"Do you know what you're getting yourself into? Have you done this kind of thing before? Do you realize Tioga Pass is 10,000 feet?" he asked with a stern look on his face.

I assured him we did and we had and we knew. To prove it, I began to recite our more recent adventures—Mount Lassen, Siskiyou County, Death Valley.

"Okay, okay," he raised his hands in surrender. "Good luck. Put this form on your dashboard, and on your return, be sure to let the ranger on duty know you made it back." As I took the form, he gave me that look a reflected both admiration and folly.

Tourists bustled past us as we unpacked the car and loaded up the bikes. By this time, we each had four panniers and a dry sack. Jim also carried the tent and a floor pump. He'd rather carry the weight of a real piece of equipment than benefit from a cheesy lightweight one.

The traffic starting out was thicker than we cared for, so I suggested a shortcut. The now-closed Tuolumne Grove Road had been replaced, but was still used by rangers. It wasn't hard to convince Jim to exchange nine miles of traffic for six miles of dirt. His dislike of traffic was great enough to make me wonder how he ever committed to these adventures.

We were all alone for the first stretch, sometimes having to make our way around toppled branches and boulders. Jim stopped.

"Wait. I want to get my bear spray out and have it ready."

"What? Here? You really think we might run into them so close to rangers' quarters?" I asked, as I thought *What a worrywart*.

We came out bear-less (whew) at the very busy Tuolumne Grove Trailhead, and startled hikers who didn't expect to see bicycles on such an arduous path. Then we had two long, sustained uppies. The first one, climbing 2,500 feet over sixteen miles, then a quick three mile, one thousand-foot descent. Unfortunately, that drop only meant we had to climb it all over again; another relentless thousand-foot slog when we were at our most tired.

Chapter 12

Lesson #18: When One Catches a Downie in the Mountains, Enjoy It 'Cuz You're Gonna Be Going Back Up Again, Sooner or Later. There was a surprise payoff, though, a mile shy of the campground, when we were at our most ragged and wondering if we could really do it. We came to a viewpoint at 8,300 feet with a sweeping panoramic view of the Sierras, El Capitan, and Half Dome. Again, the beautiful surprise reminded us why we were doing what we were doing.

By the time we got to Porcupine Campground, we had to put the tent up in the rain. We even had a little bit of hail and my fingers were freezing. Fortunately, by dinner, the storm clouds had dispersed and our wet stuff dried out fast. Dinner was a delicious, first-night affair—no-longer-frozen steak filets with potatoes and tomatoes. The first night we could count on something fresh and yummy. After that, heat, cold, crashes, critters—you name it—could sabotage the food in our panniers. That's partly why we loved to splurge on a restaurant on the way home; to celebrate the trip and make up for our meager pannier-meals.

Most campers pass up the bare-bones, no water, pit toilet, pack-in/pack-out Porcupine Campground as too rough, too far away. Mostly independent types camp here. We were in the tent by 8:30, asleep from exhaustion by nine, but a short time later, someone drove into our site with their headlights on. It took them so long to figure out that although there was no car, the site was taken so Jim got out of the tent. "Sorry, we got lost on our way here," the guy apologized and drove elsewhere. Being startled awake in the dark by late arrivals became a frustrating pattern when we stayed in campgrounds.

We set out for Tioga Pass, a day of cycling up close and personal with the wondrous beauty of glacier-scraped granite. While it was almost as long as the day before, the ascent was about half, less than 3,000 feet, though we could tell the air was thinner. Tenaya Lake first, then the myriad rock climbers on the cliffs on both sides of the lake, so fun to stop and watch. Many thought we were crazy, but I really wonder about rock climbers. Next was the bustling Tuolumne Meadows, then the crashing water of the Tuolumne River, all framed in by the Sierra peaks. We saw a number of cyclists that day, most were day trippers from Tuolumne campground, but we chatted with one loaded cyclist, a young German guy who was heading south to Los Angeles by way of Highway 395. He cluelessly propped his bike in the road and was surprised when cars honked at him as he went past. I said, "Welcome to the US," and we all laughed. As we parted Jim said, "Auf Wiedersehen," and he replied, "Cheers," so we knew he likely learned Brit English.

We stopped at Tioga Pass to take a pic at the little ranger hut that has a sign noting the elevation: 9,949 feet. A milestone for us to ride this high, Jim insisted on setting up a timed picture so both our beaming faces marked the milestone. Two miles downhill from the pass is Tioga Pass Resort with an open restaurant at the right time of day. A delicious meal inside a warm space out of the elements, cooked in a kitchen by somebody else when we're so hungry; one less meal to cook on our pathetic, little lightweight equipment in camp—oh, the joy. I should have an "I brake for restaurants" bumper sticker on my bike.

So we ate in this deep-red patina, log cabin chalet. They had pricey rooms and cabins to let, but we stopped for the food, standard American fare, but far better than anything we had in our panniers. The customers were quite a mix—elderly RVers, fit-as-a-fiddle backpackers, hard-hatted road crew workers.

Chapter 12

Our middle-aged waitress was all business, the restaurant was the only show in town. Well, from Lee Vining to Tuolumne, at least. After our long climb, their Classic—burgers and fries—hit the spot. Another two miles, and we made it to a real delight, and reward, for our efforts—Sawmill Walk-In campground. "Walk-in" means no cars. It was about a quarter mile down a sloped path. I got delight from pulling another fast one: the sign said Walk-in Only but we just pedaled around the gate and to our site.

We found a great spot about a half mile in and knew we wouldn't have any car headlights waking us up that night. The twelve campsites were strung out like a pearl necklace on a bluff high above Lee Vining Creek. As we set up, we watched how bicycle-less campers managed the walk-in. A family of four used a red wagon; a couple had a three-wheeled barrow; an older couple had two large backpacks and walking poles. There's a hierarchy to people on the road. Motor vehicles hate cyclists because we force them to slow down, pedestrians hate cyclists because we startle them when trying to pass as they walk, clueless, down the middle of a shared path. To be a cyclist is to be always on the lookout for trouble. So when we occasionally come across an advantage, it's fun to gloat. And gloat I did as I sat in my legless camping chair with a hot cup of tea and my journals, watching campers making multiple trips to their cars. The wildflowers were prolific, the most I ever remember seeing up here. Reds, violets, yellows, whites, all mostly tiny petals; they don't grow very big at this elevation, maybe because it was a cold, wet spring. We saw chipmunks and heard lots of birds. We even saw a few furry marmots—fat little buggers with squirrel-like faces and tails, and yellowish shoulders.

We liked the solitude of the campsite so much we decided to stay an extra night. Then we took off on unloaded bikes to Saddlebag Lake for a picnic and a swim. When we got to the lake, however, there was a sign saying no bicycles allowed, but horses were okay. Gain one advantage, lose another. As we were standing there steaming about the unfairness of it all, a dude in a stained baseball cap and Ben Davis jeans so dirty they were stiff bolted out of a mangled pickup and took strides a yard long toward us.

"Shitty deal, huh? I don't get it, I come up here a lot and I've complained to the rangers. Horses' hooves do much more damage than bike wheels."

Jim found the guy intriguing enough to continue the conversation, which was unusual for him, and soon they were comparing notes. As I scouted for a spot to walk the bikes down to the water, I heard the man exclaim.

"You two, on bikes, all the way up here? Why, you must be animals!" I turned to see his dude-ness lean into Jim, reach for his hand and shake it so hard I worried for Jim's shoulder socket. "Congratulations, way to go." Jim and I were equal parts shocked and pleased. We knew it was a significant achievement to reach these heights by bicycle, but by this time, it felt old hat enough we often forgot the impact our presence could have. It was sweet to be reminded in such an earnest way.

It was early so we rode down Tioga Pass Road to Lee Vining and Mono Lake. The eastern side of the Sierras is another world, an arid and desolate contrast to Yosemite, with a landscape closer to Death Valley. The dirt path to Mono Lake was too soft to bike, but the town of Lee Vining gave us an opportunity to enjoy another restaurant meal before we climbed back to Sawmill. Every restaurant was Mono this or Mono that. Jim picked Mono Cone because we could order at an outdoor window and eat around back in a shaded picnic table area. As Jim placed the order, I laughed and tapped his shoulder to point out a sign in the window — Warning: If you're smoking, you'd better be on fire.

The sun was already shining on the mountain tops to our west the next morning when we got out of the tent. It was a fifty-eight-mile ride back to the car, and then a 150-mile drive home. On a Sunday afternoon. It was gonna be a long day. So we skipped breakfast, packed in less than an hour, and timed it to arrive at Tioga Pass Resort to chow down a hearty egg breakfast the minute they opened at 8 a.m.

Later we got to do a new "biking with" — this time it was a hawk who hovered just above us for about a mile. We speculated it was spying out my pink flowered shirt for something edible. The sun was at just the right angle that the hawk's shadow was on the road right in front of us. Jim surmised it was a red-tailed hawk because of its dark gray wings and a reddish-yellow underside.

We became part of a parade; literally hundreds of noisy motorcycles, in small groups up to dozens at a time, passed us in our six-hour descent. Out for a Sunday tour? Unfortunately they deprived us of the solitude and quiet of the forest. Many would wave at us and give us a thumb's up, which Jim and I found odd. We guessed they saw us as comrades, anti-car, out-in-nature people; we had something in common. We came to dislike noisy motorcycles more than cars and whales.

Ultimately, we cycled Yosemite's Tioga Pass Road five times during our ten years of Learning How to Tour. I don't think there was ever a place that was not a repeat, a few we did only once; some two or three times. Only Yosemite did we ride five times. I only had the Garmin for our fifth and last trip but it revealed so much. Turns out the "descent" from Tioga Pass at 9950 feet to our car at the Big Oak Flat entrance, elevation 4,870 feet so you do the math. Major downie, right? Turned out the 5,000-foot descent included almost 3,000 feet of climbing. In my journals, I added new items to track. Besides miles, time, and max elevation I now followed and recorded max speed, average speed, moving time, stopped time, elevation climb, elevation descent. I loved it all. Curiously, elevation descent turned out to be most surprising. Paper maps rarely included elevation change data.

Every trip was a weighty challenge in many ways: the relentless first-day 3500-feet slog to Porcupine Campground, the second day peak at 10,000-foot high Tioga Pass, the traffic, etc., and yet it was unparalleled; traversing clear across the Sierras with extraordinary views and off-the-grid camping. Averaging eight miles an hour allowed us to intimately appreciate the unparalleled beauty of Yosemite.

East side of Tioga Pass Road

Resting after a day of climbing in Yosemite

Checking out crashing waters of Tuolomne River

View near Olmsted Point

THIRTEEN

Volcano Land

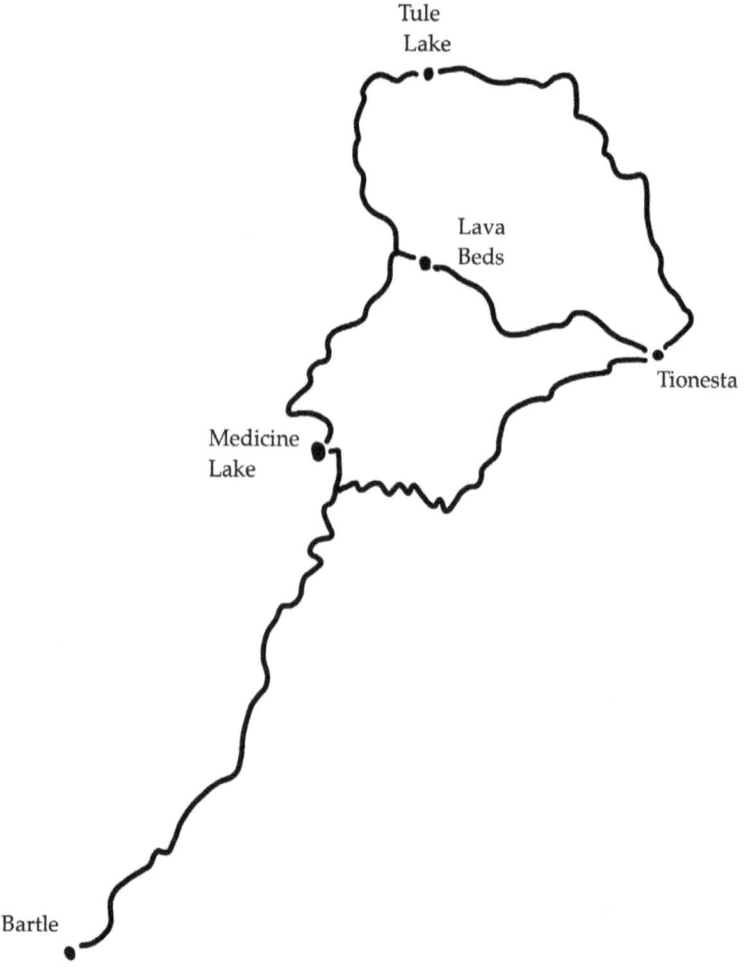

Our next trip held great sentimental significance. Back in the '80s, on our first camping trip with the kids, we pulled into PG&E's North Shore Campground on the Pit River, about an hour's drive east of Mount Shasta, and found a very rustic campground—pit toilets and water available only from an old-fashioned bright red hand pump. The kids and I found the pump such a novelty we fought taking turns to get water. Our campsite was closest to the river, so we could easily launch the canoe, and the kids—Oliver was eight, Eleanor was four—ran back and forth from the campsite to the pump and the lake.

We weren't sure we/they would like camping, so for this first trip we didn't even buy a tent, just an industrial-strength blue tarp and four totally cheesy denim sleeping bags. We thought if this trip was a go, then we'd buy a tent next year. A ranger stopped by to check on us and expressed surprise we were happy on the north side of the Pit when just across on the south side was Burney Falls State Park with hot showers, a store, visitor center, and ice cream. (Because we only arrived from the west, we didn't realize it was there, but decided to check it out the next day. The Falls, the town, and the ice cream were all great but the kids were too little to appreciate hot showers.)

"Well," he said, "if you like this place, you should head north an hour and then some, to Medicine Lake." So we did, and the rest is history. It became our favorite place to camp with the kids; we even dragged other family there for annual get-togethers.

This time, on our bikes, it would be our first just-the-two-of-us trip to Medicine Lake. The lake is really isolated and we weren't sure how much rigorous cycling we could get in if we drove all the way there, so we pulled another can-we-park-our-car deal. We stopped at Bartle Lodge on Highway 89 and went into the tidy, homey café (unusual for Northern California) for a late breakfast after our five-hour drive from home.

After we ate, I made the pitch: could we leave our car at the lodge for a few days while we biked to Medicine Lake and Lava Beds? Typically, my pitch startled the requestee into agreement. Not this time—he turned into a chatterbox we couldn't shut him up or get away from.

"Ride your bikes? From here, that's thirty miles and almost 4,000 feet higher. No, you won't make it," he insisted. He became a one-man campaign to convince us not to do this thing we were going to do, to keep us from riding. He truly thought we were crazy. It took us an hour to get his okay and extricate ourselves from his trap. "Yes, yes, we promise to be careful," we lied as we backed toward the door and quickly let ourselves out, "We promise."

We turned off Highway 89 from Bartle onto Volcanic Legacy Scenic Byway—yeah, a mouthful. The whole region northeast of Mount Shasta is a volcanic wonderland. Medicine Lake is in a caldera, a volcano that last erupted about a thousand years ago. Since then, the water flowed into the hole it left. That means the lake is up top, at 6,800 feet, and sixty miles east of Mount Shasta through a sensational landscape of vast fields of volcanic rock punctuated by stretches of mixed fir, pine, and cedar forests. There's a lot of evidence of logging, a lot of volcanic rock, not a lot of water, and not so many people. Pretty soon, we saw three deer. One had a formidable enough set of antlers that we gave them ample distance, so no "riding with this deer" today. We passed vast

Chapter 13

fields of volcanic rock with stunted trees struggling to reach their natural height in such a harsh environment.

It took us until 4 p.m. to reach Medicine Lake. All our favorite waterfront campsites were taken, so we settled in a back corner, which turned out to be a good thing for it was exceptionally windy. Being without a car or the canoe or any firewood, we opted to brave the wind to hike along the water's edge. The ranger was right all those years ago—Medicine Lake is not for the faint of heart when the wind is raging at 7,000 feet, even in summer—it's cold. The effort warmed us though, making it easier to pile in the tent for the night. The next morning, we broke camp and headed to Lava Beds National Monument.

It is a surprisingly easy and swift ride from Medicine Lake to Lava Beds. Only eighteen miles, pretty much downhill. We did it in two hours even though the road was mostly washboarded dirt. The last three miles were the hardest because the dirt got really soft and I dropped my bike. Nothing really got hurt but my pride. We picked one of the few remaining campsites with shade. This was our first time camping at Lava Beds. It gets so hot we usually just bike down for the day, but we wanted to explore a bit more and decided to gamble on the heat, especially as Medicine Lake was so windy.

After we put up the tent, we set off to tour the park. Between the caves, tubes, lava flows, Modoc War and internment camp sites, there's enough at the Lava Beds and Tule Lake to spend a week or more, but we had visited them all with the kids over the years. I would have loved to have gone into Merrill Cave—it went deep and was as cold as a refrigerator, a delicious escape in the heat, but Jim didn't want to leave our bikes unattended. So we went north to the

Tule Lake overlook. We had a lovely picnic lunch watching the birds, then Jim pitched that we return the long route, by way of Tionesta.

* * *

The hamlet of Tionesta looms large in our family camping lore. It has the closest store to Medicine Lake by many, many miles. Walking into Timber Mountain Store, a ramshackle, slanting, wooden structure that likely dates back to the nineteenth century, is like time travel. The floor has creaking planks, and if you look closely in the right light, and you can see the ground beneath.

There's a big, old, used-to-be gorgeous wrap-around bar. On both sides of the front door are freezers filled with drinks, ice, ice cream, etc. Leading up to the bar is cheap, tinny white shelves with junk food, snack food, canned food, camping supplies. Around the side and in the back is a mostly empty, dusty space that held a few tables with locally produced jewelry, cards, tchotchke kind of stuff, most covered in dust. I bought a pair of earrings there once, silver with green stones.

It didn't take much to convince me to add the miles. Beer on tap is just the best on a hot afternoon; cold bottled beer is a reasonable second, and ice cream pulls up the rear, regardless of the quality of the establishment selling it. Lesson #19: We Brake for Cold Drinks. The best cold drink on the road, usually, is beer on tap. Unfortunately, Tionesta doesn't get enough traffic, but a cold bottle or can in that heat did just fine. I'm sure they sold a lot of beer. The place was busy, five local guys filled the bar seats, so we got our beers and went outside. There was a starling nest on an eave on the porch,

Chapter 13

and every few minutes, the mother bird returned with food for her chirping babes.

A fellow with Oregon plates pulled up with "Storyteller" in big letters on his T-shirt. He got a Sierra Nevada and joined us. Turns out, he was giving the campground show that night in the amphitheater. We got ice cream for desert, said see ya later, and headed back. Boy were we pooped—seventy-three miles. I didn't want to stay awake for the show, but Jim dragged me there. Mercifully, it lasted only forty-five minutes. I struggled to stay awake sitting on a hard wooden bench, but the full moon rising behind the storyteller made it a little easier. There must have been at least thirty people there. His specialty was local Indian stories, and he told a Modoc myth about how the coyote brought fire to them.

In spite of the workout, to escape the heat the next day we headed back to Medicine Lake, hoping it would be less windy and warmer. We took the long way round, thirty-five miles through Tionesta. I could bike downhill on the dirt road, but I wasn't strong enough to bike back up it. That meant we got to have another treat in Tionesta, and Jim smartly packed a couple of cold beers deep in his pannier to enjoy that night.

We returned to our back corner campsite, and whoever stayed in our site the night before left quite a pile of firewood. Plus, it was warm enough to go for a swim, though I think I stayed in less than three minutes; the lake is about 150 feet at its deepest and it's cold. We had a huge pasta dinner (not much fresh food remained in our larder), and Jim built a great campfire with all the wood that lasted until almost 9 p.m.. At twilight, as we sat and enjoyed the fire, a nervy chipmunk climbed on our picnic table. Before I could stop him, he made off with two yellow daisies I planned to press in my journal.

Using the non-stick lid of our three-piece set the next morning, I cooked pancakes one at a time, keeping them warm in tin foil so we could eat together, a slow process, then made a fast and cool descent down to Bartle. We had another meal with the Chatterbox, suffering through another hour with him as a way to say thanks for letting us leave our car there.

We ordered burgers and fries even though it was still morning. The café was empty, so after serving us, he got himself a cup of coffee, pulled up a chair and joined us for breakfast, something I really don't like but did my best to hide. He had no questions about our ride, instead, he talked about himself. Local to the area, born and raised, he had Jim's attention when he said he was into geology and had a gold mine on the Salmon River. He would have talked all day, but eventually, I pried Jim away and we headed home via another soak at Harbin.

Enjoying an unloaded ride from Medicine Lake

Setting up camp at the end of a day

FOURTEEN

We Go Radioactive

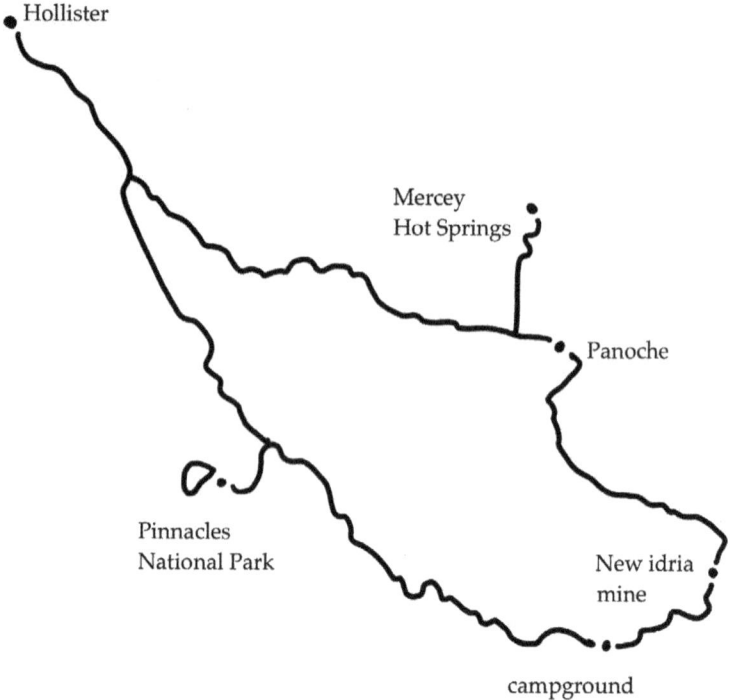

We were now in the fourth year of Learning How-To-Cycle-Tour-Independently. Both kids were now away at college and Jim got five weeks of vacation a year, but our trips still had to fit into my community college teaching schedule. As a nontenured adjunct, I cobbled together a full-time schedule teaching American and European history at three different East Bay community colleges. Jim did his best to get all his time off from the refinery during my semester breaks. After spending the two previous Easters in Siskiyou County, we turned our gaze south. This time Jim suggested San Benito County. Leaving the car in Hollister, we'd head to Pinnacles National Park. And I found Mercey Hot Springs, within a day's ride of Hollister, that allowed camping. We could do a loop and enjoy a soak on our last day.

Definitely we were getting bolder. Back then, Hollister was laid-back enough that we just left our car parked on a street near the courthouse and didn't check in with anyone; it looked safe enough. After doing some quick shopping and dining, we took Highway 25, more or less following the San Andreas Fault through a gorgeous valley still lusciously green from late spring rains.

The ranger at the entrance to Pinnacles charged us half price for our campsite because we were on bikes. But alas, we didn't do our homework—Pinnacles is noted for its hiking trails, but we forgot to bring hiking shoes for its arduous trails. The campground was quite close to the west entrance, so after setting up camp, we hopped on unloaded bikes and followed the road as long as we could, climbing up along Bear Creek as the canyon narrowed into a gulch and dead-ended at a trailhead. The creek still had water and the wildflowers were out, poppies and tipsy little yellow fiddlenecks, blues and pinks and whites. April is a great month for wildflowers in California.

We went to bed Friday night to a half-empty campground and woke to find every spot taken. It never ceases to amaze us how many people arrive and set up after dark. The sites nearest us had three families (one American and two French) on their annual spring vacations, all in pop-up vans. They were curious about our bikes. One of the Frenchmen, Luc, invited us over for some real coffee (how could I refuse?) before their kids woke up. He peppered Jim with questions in his heavily accented English about our cycling and equipment.

"I've seen families cycling loaded in France, often from one *camping municipale* to another along a dedicated route, but I don't know about doing it here. The sensibility is so different, the distances so much greater."

"Yes," Jim agreed, "so far, our longest trip has been about ten days. I'm eager to take a longer journey." Once Jim saw the telescope in the back of Luc's van, it was Jim's turn for the questions.

"Pinnacles in one of the parks in California that has a dark sky program for reducing light pollution. It's a great place for viewing," Luc said. "You can see tonight—come on over and star gaze with us."

"Oh," Jim sighed, "sorry, I'd love to, but we've only got four days this trip. How about a raincheck?" They exchanged addresses. "Maybe we'll meet up cycling in France," Jim laughed.

"Maybe, we'll see," Luc said. "You two sure are an inspiration."

Chapter 14

We didn't stick around much longer, returning to Highway 25 and stopping from time to time for Jim to get up close and personal to study the evidence of earlier earthquakes: linear fissures in the grass, jagged fences, cracks in the asphalt. I enjoyed the wildflowers and pressed some in my journal.

When we got to the intersection of Wild Ass Road, we decided to skip any of the amenities Coalinga might offer to take on a more challenging dirt road through BLM land. The road was paved most of the way to the campground, which felt just as chaotic as our first bike-camping trip, Frank Raines in Stanislaus County. But this time, instead of trial bikers, the place was filled with off-road vehicles and motor bikes. We left Pinnacles with full water bottles, but when we got to the campground, the sign said the creek water was contaminated with asbestos. That meant we had to make it through dinner, breakfast, and at least twelve miles of dirt road in the middle of nowhere to get to our next possible water source. I suggested to Jim we ask some of the other campers for water.

"Absolutely not," he replied. "I don't want to borrow from strangers and I sure don't want these characters knowing we're so ill-prepared. They'll laugh us outa town."

Men and their pride. I thought back to our first bike ride on the brand-new bike he picked out for me, in '74. We left Stone's Cyclery in Alameda and climbed up and over the Berkeley Hills. Jim wanted to show me where he rode while a student at Cal, but as we mounted Bear Creek Road with a view of Briones Reservoir I got a flat, only about twenty miles on new tires, and I got a flat. We were out there with no repair kit and Jim wanted to walk all the way back to his apartment in Berkeley, but I had other ideas and flagged down a pickup truck who dropped us off in downtown Berkeley—oh, was he embarrassed.

The bikers' heads did turn as we pulled in, incredulous. What were we, lowly cyclists, doing in their He-Man motorcycle territory? Jim didn't want to give them any extra ammunition. He was the equipment guy, after all, and water fell under equipment, not navigation. When we cased the campground for a site, we could feel the heat of all eyes on us. But when we started to set up our tent three campers came over and introduced themselves.

Mark, his girlfriend Patty, and her daughter, Chelsea, invited us to share their campfire. Over the fire, they strongly recommended we not try to ride the dirt road ahead.

"It's too hard for bicycles, plus the bikers ride up and down it all day to get to the trails, make a lot of noise, and aren't very careful or respectful." With that info, we looked at each other, connecting without a word, thanked them, but said we were going to try. We thanked them again for their hospitality and told them we were hitting the sack to get an early start.

Lesson #20: Try It; If It Turns Out to Be Too Hard, Turn Around. What we didn't tell them was how much we hated motorcycle noise. Getting up super early was one way to avoid them. Combined with our lack of water, we wanted to leave as early as we could.

In the morning, Jim had a flat—on his rear tire, of course. Unlike the front tire, the back can't be repaired without taking all the gear off first, so it takes about twice as long to fix. That added twenty minutes to our race to beat the bikers. The geology blew us away as we climbed eight miles to the 4,400-foot summit. Some parts were dense brush, some barren moonscape, Georgia O'Keefe-green with gray hills on both sides. The trails were a mess of ruts and dirt and rocks; talk about degrading a landscape, There was only a mile stretch of dirt loose enough to force me to walk. Jim walked some to keep me company, though he didn't have to. But there were lots of switchbacks and the stretches of degraded road were hard-packed so we did far better than we expected.

We made it past the most popular biker area and to the top with only one biker buzzing us — a young boy passing close enough it was obvious he was trying to knock us over. We beat all the rest of them to the punch; they were probably still sleeping off the previous night's partying. We stopped to celebrate our good fortune and enjoy the view — ridges upon ridges of the Diablo Range, and glimpses of the San Joaquin Valley. We couldn't celebrate too much, though, for we were getting alarmingly low on water with no idea where/when we could top up.

Coming down was a far greater hassle than going up. It's easier to skid out going down, plus four miles were steep with loose dirt. Jim came to a screeching halt at New Idria, an abandoned ghost/mining town with decrepit buildings, rusted metal roofs, collapsing wooden structures of uncertain function, piles of tailings defacing the hills, and a garish orange stream running down between the buildings. I was appalled and turned off by the utter destruction of the environment and all the mining waste from extracting cinnabar, an exceedingly toxic mineral that contains mercury and turns everything orange. The degradation by the off-roaders on the other side of the pass paled in comparison to this. Jim would have stayed for hours, so entranced was he by the other-worldly scene, but as a chemical engineer, he took seriously the signs that said trespassing was not allowed due to radioactive waste.

We certainly weren't going to be getting water anywhere near here, and we were still twenty miles from the dot on the map called Panoche. The question was, what was there? Would it be a town, a hamlet, or what? We were almost out of water—I had less than a cup, Jim a tad more. Jim was convinced Panoche would have a store because there were several roads that intersected it. As we coasted down the gentle downie from New Idria in the heat, we eagerly anticipated not only filling up our water bottles but maybe scoring an ice cream. But alas, there was nothing there. Not a town, not a hamlet, zip. *Greatly despondent* is an understatement. Two miles later, we passed a school where I was certain we could tap an outdoor water fountain if one of us hopped the six-foot-high fence, but not only wouldn't Jim do it, he forbade me. Oh, we had a big fight, but he wouldn't budge. He was sure somebody would come along and arrest us if we ignored the big No Trespassing signs.

We drank the last of our water, and a paranoia set in—it was another eight miles to the hot springs, and I didn't call in advance (this was before cell phones.) What if the place was closed? Plus, the area was parched, all brown and dry, no creeks. (Not that Jim would want to filter water from a creek around here with what we just pedaled past.) If the hot spring was closed, we wouldn't even be able to free-camp without water. Oh, I was freaking out.

"Jim," I admitted ruefully as I slowed down to let him catch up to me, "at the intersection up ahead we've got a tough choice: take the eight miles north to the hot spring, though I forgot to call and verify they were open yet, OR we can stay heading west, and it's probably twenty-nine miles to the next place with water, Paicines."

"What?" Jim braked to a halt. "Whaddya mean you forgot to call?" We were both pretty parched, the temperature was in the low eighties, and though I forgot to call Mercey,

Chapter 14

I did remember that the twenty-nine miles to Paicines required a 2,000-foot climb, though I did not reveal that detail just now. "Let's decide when we get to the intersection," Jim suggested.

Then, just as we slowed to a stop at Oliver Road, the intersection for Mercey, we spied a sign, "Cold Beer ½ mile." The hell with hot springs, we made a beeline to find a funky, dusty roadside bar that had a wooden sidewalk, two hitching posts, sitting in the middle of a huge—but empty—parking lot. We entered and found a bar with dollar bills hanging from the ceiling, a balding, greasy-haired bartender in jeans, white T-shirt and black leather vest, and a scrawny, already intoxicated peroxide-blond older woman wearing Easter-bunny ears. They had Budweiser on tap, and it was so delicious Jim had two mugs. I had one and we split a fourth. Plus, they had peanuts at the bar and a cook ready to serve in the kitchen, at 11 in the morning—Easter morning. We ordered two hot turkey and cheese sandwiches with fries on the side. Then the bunny-eared lady came tottering over, said, "Happy Easter" and offered each of us a colored hard-boiled egg from her Easter basket. They made great hors d'oeuvres with the peanuts, washed down by the beer, as we waited for our warm sandwiches to arrive. Life was good—suddenly so good! It wasn't lost on me that this was yet another epic Easter-break adventure!

When we bid the bar adieu and made our way back to Oliver Road, I started singing "On Top of Old Smokey" as I deliberately zig-zagged from one edge of the road to the other. I still can't figure out how that song about meatballs turning into trees percolated up. I'm guessing the last time I sang it might have been at Girl Scout Camp when I was twelve. Then I started laughing so hard I had to stop riding.

I had a ball singing my lungs out the eight miles to Mercey, even though we weren't worried about bears, and Mercey was open.

The office was in a dilapidated, adobe-church-like structure. We had our choice of tent sites and picked the only one with shade. There was a ten-sided, ten-person tub at 105 degrees and an 85 degree swimming pool. They had two private bathtubs for an additional ten dollars an hour. We went straight to the hot tub and, oh, it felt so good. A Kathy Bates lookalike and a family of four were already there, chatting away. Jim closed his eyes so as to appear to be sleeping—that way he didn't have to talk.

I got out of the tent early the next morning and made a beeline for the hot tub. A half-moon rose over my right shoulder as I watched the sky turn from gray to pale pink to blue. Yesterday's mom was already there; "Kathy Bates" joined shortly. The family had recently moved from Idaho to San Jose, and Kathy Bates was originally from Washington, so we ended up talking hot springs—they both had extensive experience soaking in their home states. They competed notes over not only which state had more, but whose were better.

"Doesn't matter," Kathy said, "there are so many of them you should try both states." I made a mental note to share this info with Jim.

We made breakfast the next morning, broke camp, and went for another soak before taking on the forty-seven miles to Hollister. The air was brisk and the wind was picking up. It got bad enough Jim offered to ride in front, and I was surprised how much easier it is to pedal with someone in front. We biked ten miles into a strong headwind while climbing 2,000 feet to get over Panoche Pass. Menacing

Chapter 14

storm clouds appeared and we were already hungry at ten-thirty, so we stopped to layer up and chow down on tuna sandwiches before the rain hit us. An odd, orchid/tulip-like flower, mostly white but with an interesting pattern of red, black, and yellow-orange inside distracted us from the rain as we ate. The rain and wind continued up and over the pass, then eased up for the downie to Hollister.

The geology on this ride was a rich story of contrasts and kept the two of us entertained through valleys, over ridges, along escarpments, around mines. Jim's interest in geology piqued by all our cycling, he now made a habit of carrying geology books. On this trip, Jim stopped me more than once to point out and study the scars of past earthquakes (the Hollister area has a lot of them). San Benito County seemed to possess every climate and geology zone in the state. We were never bored.

Back in Hollister, Jim picked out the Hard Times Café on San Benito Street and we had a second lunch of burgers and fries. The ride home brought more rain and wind, but we mostly ignored it inside our nice warm car.

"What a trip," Jim exclaimed. "Another great adventure. I can't decide what was the most remarkable part—the horrible quality of Clear Creek Road, and we climbed it in spite of all the naysayers, New Idria, the bar, the hot springs—I love the element of surprise."

Yes, I thought. *He sure does, much more than* I do. "I don't like surprises as much as you," I replied. "I much prefer having an idea of where we're going. But you're right, this trip was remarkable for the incredible diversity and number of surprises. And we sure showed those naysayers what we're made of."

Near Pinnacles

Abandoned New Idria mining town, note the orange creek water

FIFTEEN

*Anne & Jim Become an Item,
and Take Their First Big Adventure*

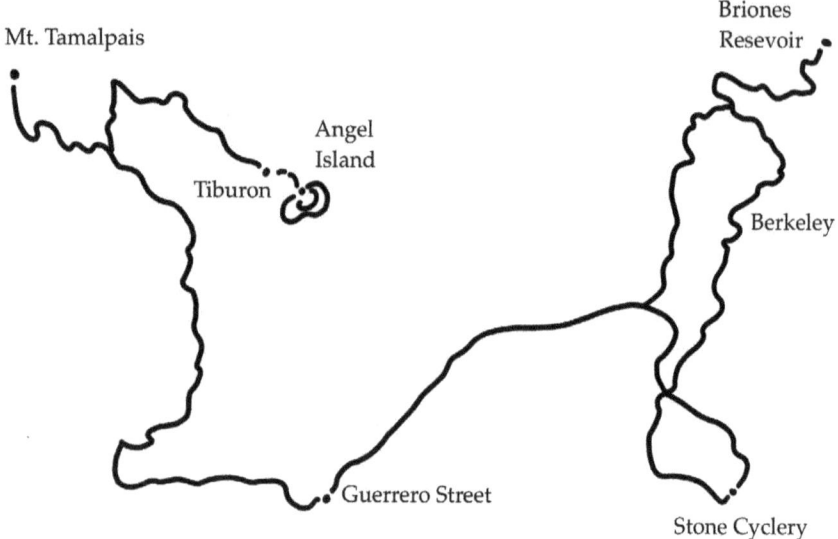

I met Jim on a sunny Sunday morning in mid-September 1973. Energized from soccer practice at Balboa Park on one of the few women's teams in the city, I bounded up the stairs two steps at a time. Jim was standing on the top landing chatting with Robert, his friend from Cal and my new landlord/roommate. It was not an auspicious beginning—he made a crack about my uniform that I misinterpreted as an insult so I made a hasty retreat.

The first of the month, I'd rented the front bedroom on the third and top floor of a sunny, still-in-mint-condition, seven-room Victorian flat at Guerrero and 17th Street. It was big and spacious, with off-white walls accenting the gorgeous original mahogany woodwork and moldings. The lease was in Robert's name, and he rented out the various rooms to whomever felt like a good match. I lived there eighteen months and it was a transformative experience for me—but that's not the story here.

Jim lived in Berkeley and visited Robert regularly. For months, whenever he showed up, I would disappear into my room and close the door. He was twenty-six with blue eyes, tall, painfully thin (I think he often forgot to eat—probably the lack of coins in his pockets reinforced his forgetfulness) with really, really curly hair, even curlier than mine. I was nineteen. After that first awkward introduction, it took six months for each of us to learn from Robert that the other was interested. Robert the matchmaker finally connected us in March. Once we did, we hit it off. Jim was into science and art and movies, and I was into history and art and movies. We had a lot to talk about, and within minutes, we learned we both also shared a love of cycling.

Once we made the bike connection, the first order of business, according to Jim, was to get me a new bike. Shortly after my arrival in San Francisco, my brother Jack came down from Sacramento (to check out my living arrangements and report back to my parents) and brought with him a clunker of a bike. It was pathetic, but it moved when I pushed on the pedals. Jim didn't like it.

"It's gotta go, there's no way you'll enjoy riding the East Bay hills with me on that," he insisted. So I took the AC Transit over the Bay Bridge to meet him at Stone Cyclery in Alameda, where I could get a better bike with low gears. He picked out a Schwinn Le Tour for $160, a lot of money at the time, but considering I rode it for twenty-five years, I got my money's worth. He rode his bike to Alameda so we could break in my new purchase up and over the Berkeley Hills. Later, as we climbed along Briones Reservoir, I got a flat and Jim didn't bring a repair kit.

"We can walk back," he said sheepishly, "it's not that far."

"The hell it ain't, all the way up Wildcat Canyon?" I replied, waving my hand up toward the hills.

"Well, what else are we gonna do? There's no buses out here," he insisted.

"Hitchhike, of course," I announced.

Needless to say, Jim was not happy with that idea, but we were eight hilly miles from his apartment. As he bent down to see if there was any way he could repair my flat, I waved down the first vehicle that passed us, a pickup. I took that as a sign—the first vehicle was a truck with an empty bed, AND it stopped. Jim barely spoke in the truck, but he cheered up when the guy dropped us off at Shattuck and University. We walked our bikes to the Missing Link bike store where he bought a patch kit and fixed the bike on the sidewalk.

* * *

It turned out that Jim also acquired his first ten-speed bike in high school, in San Diego. His was also a Christmas present, but, ever the mechanic, he remembered the make and model. A Rafaël Géminiani (a postwar Tour de France racer turned bike builder). His new bike coincided with a girlfriend relocating from Ocean Beach to Solano Beach, twenty miles north. There was no freeway in the early sixties, and the single-lane coastal roads ran through mostly farmland. Jim didn't have enough money to pay for gas, but he could pedal. The relationship didn't survive his move north to Cal, but his love of bikes did. (While a student at Cal, he discovered the East Bay back roads.)

We quickly became inseparable. Neither of us had much money, so we got around by bikes, buses and ferries. Jim was keen to backpack Yosemite, and he proposed we go together. When I said yes, he booked tickets on the Greyhound bus that ran to the valley.

"I don't want to stick around here tonight, there's too way many people," Jim said as the shuttle driver tossed a mountain of backpacking gear for the passengers to sort at the Tuolumne Meadows Visitors Center. So after twenty minutes of jostling, we strapped on our rented gear (loaded with four days' provisions) and headed south toward Cathedral Peak. Several hours later, we found a shaded grove with a creek nearby and decided to call it a day. After dinner, Jim diligently followed the recommendations in his Yosemite High Sierra Hiking Guidebook, piling all of our food into one backpack and slinging it over a high branch of a tree fifteen feet up and about thirty feet from our tent, to keep out of reach of the bears.

We were too tired to collect wood, much less build a campfire, and tired enough to hit the sack early, so we piled into the tent at dusk. Within minutes, we heard growling and rumblings outside, then crashing, snarling, and breaking branches.

"What's that?" I shrieked as Jim scrambled to find his flashlight, fumbled with the zipper and went out in the darkness. I wasn't remotely interested in heading out of the safety of our fortress, er, tent.

"There's three of them," Jim yelled as he entered the tent. "I saw three sets of eyes, probably a mom and two babies. And they've already got the backpack down on the ground and they're ripping it to shreds." For about ten minutes, we both sat in the tent terrified, listening to growls, rips, and thrashing. Jim was keen to go out again while I was frozen in my sleeping bag, not wanting to move. We slept fitfully, taking turns at sleeplessness, debating what to do.

"Let's pack up and leave," Jim said at one point, "try to find a safer place, away from the bears."

"NO way," I shrieked. "No way you're getting me out of this tent in the dark. If we have to die, if the bears are gonna eat us, they're gonna have to come get me, I'm not going to them."

With first light, we assessed the damage. It was chaos at the base of the tree where Jim had so confidently tied up the backpack. All our food was gone, *poof*. Even the tins of canned meat were ripped open with raw sharp metal edges, licked clean; not one shred of meat left. The only container that had not been consumed by the bears was one yet-to-be-opened bottle of wine. Everything else was g-o-n-e.

"No food in the tent," Jim's guidebook had advised, and

he insisted we pile it all in the strung-up-in-the-trees backpack. But I couldn't admit I wasn't comfortable spending a night without food—what if I got hungry? I'd surreptitiously hid two candy bars and a packet of lemonade mix in my gear in the tent.

"What? You did what?" Jim was not happy when I told him we had something to eat that morning. "They might have attacked us in the tent, then where'd we be? Don't ever do that again."

After our meager breakfast, we anxiously rushed out of that campsite with no idea of what was going to happen next. Well, I knew what I wanted to happen next—I wanted to stop the first people we saw, cry on their shoulders, and ask for some food. Jim?

"I don't want to ask for help," Jim announced as we broke down camp. "We're strong enough to make it to the valley by dark, there's plenty of water along the trail."

One, two, eight, twelve, fifteen, finally—ugh, ugh, ugh—*nineteen* miles we hiked, down, down, down to the valley. The final few miles were the hardest, reminding me of my first big bike ride home from Stephentown in '70. We tramped past so many great spots we planned to savor. With Jim's insistence on not asking for help, if we didn't get back to the valley, we'd have to spend a food-less and sleep-less night in the tent—and what if there were bears again? We really had to make it to the valley that night.

Discouraged and exhausted, we finally made it back four days earlier than we planned. We changed our return bus tickets, and when Jim sheepishly returned the rented backpacks the guy was really nice about it. He didn't even charge Jim extra.

"Comes with the territory," he laughed. "The number of Yosemite hikers who run into bears . . . we keep a seamstress on staff." He laughed.

Ten months after our first meeting and three months into becoming An Item, our first great adventure revealed several things: Yosemite was utterly and addictively beautiful, bears or no bears. We'd go back again soon, and often. And this fiasco didn't divide us; rather it bonded us in a deeper way than we expected so early in our relationship. There'd be many more trips, many more fiascoes, many more learning experiences, bonding experiences. We're still together as I write this, forty-seven years later. But I'll tell ya one thing, I haven't been backpacking since.

Berkeley Hills view of San Pablo Resevoir

Yosemite Valley

Top of Yosemite Falls

Mirror Meadow

Top of Yosemite Falls

SIXTEEN

Beyond California #1: Blown Away

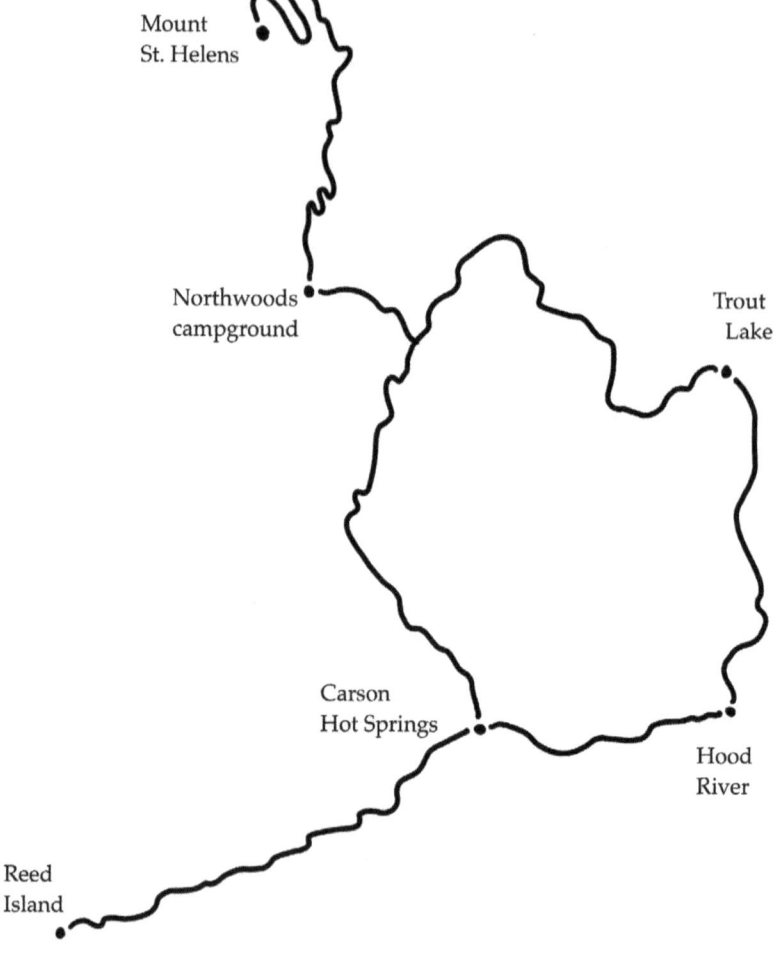

We settled on the Columbia River for our first out of California adventure because we were keen to do another follow-the-river route. We only had ten days, so we were pushing it a bit. The drive was too long for us to do in a day, which meant we'd have to spend two nights, coming and going, in motels. That'd leave only six, seven days tops, for cycling. The plan was to follow the Columbia upriver and maybe on to the Snake at Kennewick, if we had time.

Jim suggested we stay at the Motel 6 in Yreka, he remembered it was across the street from the Black Bear Diner, where we ate after our soggy last day in Siskiyou.

"We can check in and have dinner in the diner—remember how delicious the berry pie was?" Our obsession with food knew no bounds; our hunger led us to accept fare of lower quality on the road than what we usually enjoyed in the Bay Area.

We arrived at Beacon Rock, a state park high on a bluff overlooking the Columbia River. We lucked out and got a nice, tidy site in a thick and green wooded thicket of moss-covered logs and happy ferns in the undergrowth. After setting up camp, we walked to the top of Beacon Rock for the view of the river we'd be cycling along tomorrow. As we passed a friendly youngish ranger mowing the lawn of a (marked) private residence littered with kids' toys, he paused to wipe his brow.

"Hello," he said. "Enjoy the view up there?"

"Oh yes," I piped up, and then taking advantage of his friendly nature and with ulterior motives, I asked if we might be able to leave our car with him. Ten minutes later, after promising him our car did not leak oil, he gave his okay for us to leave our car in his driveway for a week.

Saturday morning we quietly parked our car without disturbing the ranger or his family and headed out on our loaded-up bikes on the Washington side of the river. Soon, there were stretches of the river with dozens of bobbing, brightly colored sails. Like surfers on Sonoma County's coast, windsurfers on the Columbia have ways of knowing when the wind is ideal. Unfortunately for us, the fierce wind coming down the gorge and heading out to the Pacific made a brutal headwind for us.

"Stop," Jim called out, "This isn't working. We've got to figure out an alternative." I was so disappointed. But Jim was right, the headwind was brutal. What to do?

"We just passed a visitor center, maybe a half mile back," I reluctantly offered. "Let's turn back and see if we can find a road away from the wind."

"Yeah," Jim replied. "Maybe if we head north or south we can get out of this wind tunnel."

We turned back to a sunny little kiosk. Jim guarded the bikes while I went inside. They had a terrific poster-size map of Skamania County for two bucks. It included icons for campgrounds, lakes, forests, and parks, so I bought it.

"Let's head north." I conceded our river plan as I spread the map out on a picnic table where Jim was waiting for me. "Look, there's a lot of campgrounds, and Mount St. Helens is in the northwest corner of the county. Maybe there'll be less wind in the woods and we can make it to the volcano. It'd be a trip to see the scar."

"Fine," Jim said, trusting my judgment without even looking at the map. And just like that, our plans changed. We turned north and stopped in the quaint town of White

Salmon where we loaded up on groceries. I knew food and restaurant options would be slimmer in the boondocks.

Back in the saddle with well-stocked panniers, we found the woods a great buffer. The thick green paradise was a fave of mosquitoes—they, too, liked to get out of the wind. We got out of the wind but now we'd spend the next week being eaten alive. A silver lining was the traffic was light compared to California—pit toilets are a real tourist deterrent. And the pokey little towns were a delight. We stopped at a hamburger joint in the town of Trout Lake and ate outside at picnic tables shaded by bright red-and-white-striped umbrellas. The perky waitress greeted us in a matching striped outfit.

"We're noted for our local huckleberry products," she offered before Jim or I had even decided what we wanted. "And we sell jellies and jams to go, too, but I guess you guys won't be interested in the frozen berries," she laughed. I skipped the fries to make room for a slice of pie with my burger, but Jim went the distance.

"Give me a milkshake with my burgers and fries, and I'll follow up with a slice of pie, but not à la mode."

"Are you sure? Think about all the calories you burn on the bike," she suggested as she turned to hand the order to the chef.

Later that day, we pulled into Goose Lake campground. It had a thick, thick pine forest coming right down to the water's edge, and though cold, was great for swimming—especially as we had been without showers for a few days. Our closest neighbors took pity on us and not long after we finished setting up our tent.

Gary and Alice waved first and then sidled on over. They told us they were retired and liked to drive their fifth wheel over to the forest for a change from their arid home in Kennewick. I had the feeling they were overly bored with each other and were keen for diversion.

"Why don't the two of you join us for our campfire after dinner?" asked Gary.

"Yes, we've got lots of firewood," added Alice. "It'll be nice to have company." I knew immediately Jim's reply would be no so I piped up.

"We'd love to. We picked up a local bottle of dry white wine in Trout Lake we can bring with us." Jim gave me the eye as I skipped back to our campsite to prepare dinner.

Two hours later when Jim offered them some of our wine Gary replied, "If you like whiskey save the wine for yourselves tomorrow. Would either of you like whiskey? I can give it to you straight up or with Coke."

As we both declined, Jim poured wine in our very beat-up Little Mermaid mugs (a sentimental favorite for me, we'd used them since we camped with the kids. I was Flounder and Jim was Sebastian.) Back around the time we began camping as a family, Eleanor had a classmate who gave her a promotional set of quality plastic (is that a self-canceling phrase?) Disney mugs and they became part of our camping equipment. We re-appropriated our two mugs into our bike-camping gear. After being offered whiskey, I was a little embarrassed about drinking out of such childish cups. Sensing what I was thinking Alice laughed.

"Looks like your cups have done a fair amount of camping." Our laughter broke the ice and we had a pleasant visit. They were easy and mellow and gave us tips for camping in the state, although we tried to tell them we only had days, not months. We didn't last much past dark and the next morning we were gone before they even came out of their camper.

Chapter 16

Two days later, we tried to conquer Mount St. Helens on its east side.

"We have two choices tomorrow," I told Jim. "If we take everything with us, we can free-camp tomorrow night, or we could leave our gear here and cycle unloaded. If we do that, we can go farther and faster, but we'll have to climb and return in one day."

Jim thought about it and said, "Aren't there any campgrounds on the way up? If not, I'm not sure I like the idea of us free-camping on the slopes of a mountain prone to blowing its top. What if it blows while we're hidden? No one will know. No, I'd rather try to make it unloaded and come back the same day." So it was settled, the threat of volcanic activity intimidated both of us. We left our tent at Swift Reservoir campground and would return the next night.

Forest Road 25 went due north and climbed a ridge on the east side of a valley, allowing us panoramic views of Mount St. Helens and its devastated slopes. Just before we turned off on Forest Road 99, we came across an unusual sight—another couple cycling, loaded, like us. On a tandem bike, David (a Brit) and Maiwenn (French) were twelve months into an eighteen-month national parks tour. It was a little embarrassing for Jim and I; we had more gear on our two bikes for a week than they had on their tandem for eighteen months. We exchanged pleasantries, and when I commented on the plastic peanut butter jar in one of their water holsters, they exclaimed how much they loved this most American treat, and swore by it for energy boosts.

When we compared notes, David said, "Our strategy for sustaining the physical demands of long-distance cycling is we never pedal more than five hours a day." It took me awhile to understand what he said.

"What do you mean, 'never'? How is that possible? What if five hours hits in the middle of a city or a desert?" I found his not only rigid, but ridiculous, and my tone revealed it. And his irritation showed.

"It's not hard, we just pay attention to the clock and to the maps. And if we have to, we stop early." Maiwenn stayed quiet. I'm not sure if it was because she wasn't sure of her English or she wasn't in total agreement. I found him about 180 degrees different from Jim and I, insisting wherever they were at five hours they could/would manage to find a place to free-camp for the night within yards of where they stopped. (Some days, it felt like Jim took five hours to pick a place to free-camp.)

Another strategy; they almost always free-camped and insisted it was easy. In fact, they said it was the only way they could afford to spend eighteen months cycle touring. In twelve months, they could count on one hand the number of times they paid for accommodations. We bid adieu and the experienced duet left us newbies with a lot of food for thought.

Unfortunately, the sunny day turned gray during our chat. By the time we were within ten miles of Windy Ridge, the clouds were so thick and low we had visibility of about ten feet. It'd been more than four hours since we left camp, so we decided to turn around. Even if we got to Windy Ridge, in this pea soup we wouldn't see anything more than what we could see here—gray clouds. That's when we realized it was a mistake not to have brought our gear.

Lesson #21: Things That Seem Scary at a Distance Aren't So Bad Up Close. There were plenty of places we could have free-camped and completed our assault on what was left of the volcano tomorrow. But we lost that option. As it was, we spent eight hours in the saddle, and oh, we were tired when

Chapter 16

we returned to the campground, but we gave it our best. Jim and I had come to terms with letting go when the circumstances said to let go.

That night in the tent, I noticed an icon on the Skamania County map for Carson Hot Springs. It was on the fold, and hard to read, but there it was. And it was on the way back. We got a late start the next morning, still worn out from the previous day's exertion. It's curious the different configurations hot springs cobble together to be viable businesses. Carson combined a golf course with its hot springs and hotel—that was a first for us. In an old white Victorian building, individual clawfoot bathtubs were available for short-term private rental. We both started with a scrumptious private soak and then headed to a modern building with a wall of windows that had a large warm pool and a smaller cold pool, both looking out on the golf course. It wasn't Harbin, but it was an unexpected and sweet way to end the week.

In the morning, we loaded up the car and Jim said, "Let's drive up the gorge a ways to see what we missed. I'd rather do that than check out Portland." I was pleased; it's so much fun to cover distance fast in a car after days of bicycle travel. The transition from the thick forest to the arid desert was dramatic, and happened right before The Dalles. The Maryhill Museum was closed, but Jim agreed to lock the bikes long enough for us to walk around an outdoor Stonehenge replica, sitting high on a barren brown bluff with a sweeping view of the Columbia River, green to the west and brown to the east. The clock was ticking, though—it was 600 miles to home.

"What a trip," Jim commented as we pulled on to the freeway. "But the wind—we've gotta figure a strategy around it."

"Paying attention to weather forecasts would go a long way," I volunteered, "but you know there was a lot to recommend Skamania County. I loved how off-the-beaten path it was and so few cars . . . it was freeing."

"I wish we had made it to Windy Ridge Viewpoint. And leaving our gear behind, such a mistake. What if the next day had been clear. Imagine what we would have seen, that blown-off mountain," Jim said wistfully.

"But don't you think we woulda had a really hard time sleeping out there, alone, imagining what the volcano might do?"

"Nah, we woulda gotten used to it. We'll have to come back."

"In a car!" I laughed as I gazed out the window at Mount Hood.

Columbia River

East side Mt. St. Helens

Multnomah Falls

SEVENTEEN

Beyond the US #1: Pedalers' Paradise

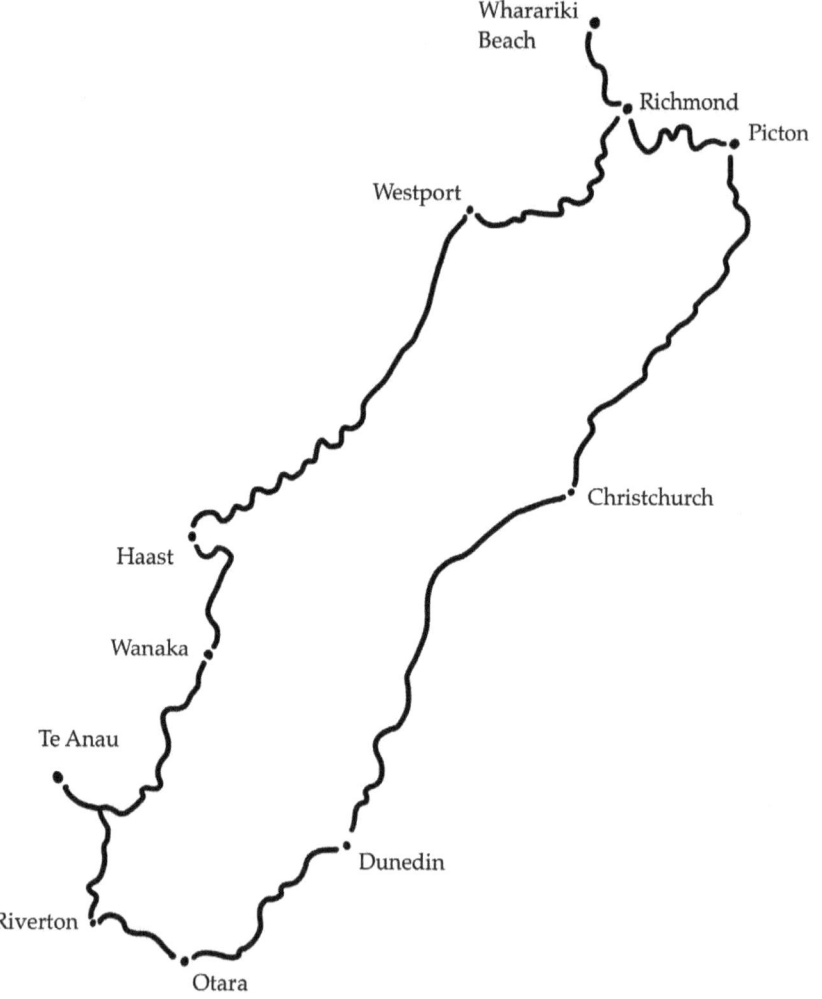

After years of trial and error, Jim had pretty much got our equipment to where he wanted it. It was a true labor of love for him, searching out and tweaking the best of the best. We learned the difference between *water resistant* and *waterproof*. Jim replaced the bought-on-sale, permeable, water-resistant canvas panniers and handlebar bags with the real deal, top-of-the-line, truly waterproof Ortlieb's from Germany—a game changer. Now he proposed another new, revolutionary modification. He wanted to slice our bikes.

And Mr. Spontaneity wanted to go somewhere completely new and different.

"I found an interesting guidebook online and I ordered it." he dropped another bomb on me one spring morning in 2002. "It's called *Pedalers' Paradise*, written by Nigel Rushton who claims the South Island of New Zealand is the best place in the world to tour by bicycle." To say I was shocked is an understatement. I saw so many red flags. For one thing, we'd have to go during my winter break, when it was summer Down Under. If we left the day after the fall semester ended and got back for the second week of the spring semester, we'd have thirty-five days; five weeks. Exactly Jim's annual vacation allotment. But that meant leaving Oliver and Eleanor, twenty-two and nineteen, for the holidays; something I hadn't done since they were born.

"Why don't we wait a few more years, until they're both done with college? I don't feel good abandoning them at Christmas," I pleaded.

"No," he said firmly. "We're not getting any younger." I was surprised by his vehemence. Then he brought up another challenge, the problem of transporting bicycles by airplane. Most people who flew their bikes packed them in bike shop's discarded oversized cardboard boxes, but there were a couple of problems. First, airlines charge extra for oversized cargo, and sometimes refuse if a flight is overbooked. Second, leaving the box in storage at the airport or hotel can be expensive and the boxes might disappear. So some just throw the boxes away upon arrival and then waste a day finding new boxes before their departure.

All this was far too messy and unpredictable for Jim. Unbeknownst to me, he spent hours searching for alternatives and found a new high-falutin' technology, "S and S Coupling," out of Roseville, a suburb of Sacramento. Jim explained what having our bikes "sliced" meant: A specialist cuts the frame in two places and welds a stainless-steel, high-tech bolt that allows the frame to be threaded and unthreaded into two pieces. The genius of it is the bikes can then be packed into standard-sized canvas bags. That means no extra handling charges, no finding and storing boxes, and the canvas bags could be rolled up and carried in our panniers—we'd be fully independent and able to fly into one airport and out of another.

"It's gonna be great, Anne," he explained as he showed me the pictures online of the process. "Really, you'll see. Trust me. We're gonna be able to go all kinds of places once we get the bikes sliced."

"I don't know," it sounded too new and too pricey, made me nervous. "How long have they been doing it, and how much is it gonna cost?"

"Don't worry about the money, you worry too much. You'll see, it'll pay for itself in a few flights." And so he wore me down. Jim's an instant gratification/perfectionist kinda

CHAPTER 17   181

guy, while I'm a pennywise/pound-foolish kinda gal. He told me I could pick out the new colors for our bikes since they'd have to be repainted. I chose a cherry burgundy for me and a cerulean blue for Jim. That was fun, perusing color swatches in a machine shop in downtown Oakland.

* * *

Ten months after he first proposed the idea, we left the kids and boarded a fourteen-hour flight to Auckland, New Zealand, on December 17, 2002. Again, our style of travel repeated itself: we had fly-in and fly-out dates, plus tickets to get to the South Island the scenic way—a train from Auckland to Wellington then a ferry across Cook Strait to Picton. Everthing else TBD.

Unfortunately, because of difficulty booking the train and ferry tickets, we decided to wait until Picton to assemble the bikes. Let me explain. In 2002, airline tickets included two free checked bags, one free carry-on, and one personal item. Thanks to the high-tech coupling, our bikes and all their parts fit into two standard canvas bags, 26" x 26" x 10", but that left everything else—clothes, gear, books—to fit in the carry-on and personal luggage: we each had four bags to handle. It wasn't too bad at the airport with the carts, but I booked a shuttle to our first nights' accommodation and the shuttle stopped three blocks away. Pure torture, three blocks.

"This isn't working, Jim. It's killing me to carry all this stuff," I yelled.

"We should have taken a taxi from the airport. How much did we save on the shuttle? I wish you weren't so cheap, Anne," he snorted. That shut me up. "Maybe we should just stop right here and assemble the bikes."

"Problem with that," I huffed as I stopped to shift the sacks once again, "we don't have reservations for bikes on the Transcenic train or the Interislander ferry. We'd have to break them back down again."

"It's obvious we didn't think through the logistics this trip," Jim tried to cheer me up. "But we're still learning and we'll do better on the next one."

After a day exploring Auckland, we booked a taxi to take us to the train station. But when beat-up white sedan pulled up Jim, and I looked at each other—no way was this gonna work. Seeing the look on our faces, the driver piped up as he approached us:

"No worries, we can fit the big bags in my boot," he said, trying to reassure us as he circled around and popped his trunk. He froze after he opened the boot. We rushed over to see a used aluminum sink. I'm thinking *We gotta find another cab quick*; we only had an hour to get to the station before our train departed. Jim did his best to help the driver jostle our cases like jigsaw puzzle pieces around the sink in the boot and in the back seat of the sedan. Twenty minutes later, we were on our way with me sitting on Jim's lap in the front seat, trying my best to keep the shifter from banging into my knees.

"Thanks for having faith in me," the driver said. "I forgot the sink was back there. A contractor friend gave it to me when a customer refused it, wrong color. Now I get one at no cost." He told us he had only lived in New Zealand for two-and-a-half years; he migrated from Ghana on the points system. I was anxious about getting to the train station, but I couldn't resist peppering him with questions about how the point system worked.

"I had to accumulate 100 points before they'd let me immigrate. They give points for age, younger is better; having family members already here, my brother migrated five years ago; employment offers, my brother got me an offer to drive this taxi; and so on."

Once our train departed, we were told to prepare for delays. The forecast was hot enough that the narrow gauge rails would likely overheat, and depending on how long it took for temps to lower, we would have to "sit on the tracks" for a while. We departed Auckland at 7:30 in the morning, the posted schedule said we were due to arrive in Wellington eleven hours later, at 6:30 p.m. I wondered how late it could possibly get?

There was a festive mood on the train—it was December 23rd, so pretty much everyone—and the train included Kiwis, Aussies, Brits, and Saffers (South Africans)—was on holiday. I followed the lead of those in the know and got "snacks on track"; two coffees and a cheese and fruit platter. We had opened a bottle of wine the night before but were too tired to drink it, so before we left the guesthouse, I poured it into one of our water bottles. After we finished our coffees, we used the cups to enjoy the wine with the cheese. It was only eleven or so, but the party was on.

We soon entered the national park and skirted around the flank of the largest mountain in New Zealand, Ruapehu (an active volcano). The view got greener and greener; deep river gorges, swamps and lava flows, and sheep everywhere. Just as we got due west of the volcano, we climbed up the Raurimu Spiral—an engineering marvel including three hairpin turns and a complete circle. On paper, the track route looks rather like the squiggle Harold drew with his purple crayon on the cover of Crocket Johnson's book. Everyone went to the windows to take pictures, four times, those in the front cars could take pictures of those in the back, and vice versa.

Sure enough, at about 3 p.m., we spent an hour on the south flank of the volcano starting and stopping before we came to a grinding halt. So odd. Because of the heat, there we were on train tracks that were being treated tenderly like a baby's bottom. Finally, the train came to a full stop at the town of Taihape, and the engineer announced we would sit for one to two hours until the air temperatures dropped enough for the wheels to ride along the tracks without melting them.

"Why don't they rip out the tracks and put in new ones of more durable material?" I asked Jim. As he shrugged, the Aussie behind me answered.

"The train is losing money; natives hardly use it, preferring their cars. Mostly, it's tourists and there's not enough to cover costs. Frankly, you're lucky you're on it—they may be completely shutting it down soon." The train stops where it did because Taihape is close enough to walk to.

"Let's mosey on over and see if we can get a real meal," Jim suggested. Alas, everyone else had the same idea. Taihape had a bit of a Wild West feel—the streets were broad and many of the stores had wide, covered wooden sidewalks. Everyone bought takeaway; no one was willing to run the risk of missing the train. While the train appeared polished and modern on the website, the reality was rather shabby chic. Thanks to the delay, our expected eleven-hour trip turned into fourteen hours. We pulled into Wellington Station at 9:30 p.m. At least our guest house was well versed with delays and was prepared to welcome us when we arrived via taxi past 10 p.m.

Chapter 17

The next morning, we easily fit our bags in a much roomier taxi driven by an older, friendly Kiwi who took us down Wellington's main street. Decorations for the grand opening of the *Lord of the Rings* movie were still up. We drove under a gigantic gold ring—fifteen feet in diameter, easy—poised high above the middle of the street in front of the theater. And reaching out from behind the roof of the building across the street was a twenty-foot-long spindly gray arm with Gollum's itching fingers just inches from the shiny gold.

The three-plus-hour passage on the ferry was a treat and a party. Yesterday's delays were forgotten in the cool sea air. We were getting closer to our goal—getting on the bikes. We pushed our eight bags in the furnished carts straight to a quiet corner of the parking lot and began unpacking the bags and assembling the bikes. Jim had practiced at home, multiple times, and it took four hours. I did my best to copy him laying out bike parts on the asphalt and hooking up what I could. With only one set of tools, some assembly had to be left to Jim, so I put myself to good use and walked downtown, got cash at a bank, and shopped for groceries.

By the time I returned, Jim had the bikes assembled. We stuffed our gear in the panniers and pedaled away—*not*. As I leaned on my handlebars, they dropped six inches. If they bike wasn't so heavy, I might have gone over the front. Floored, Jim immediately yanked out the tools.

"Oh, I forgot to tighten your stem," Jim whispered. "Too many details. Sorry, Anne, I want to go over every part of the bikes again at the campground. How far is it?"

"It's only a mile. Follow me. It'll be quick and you can get to work," I reassured him as I worried about my bike holding together for that mile.

There are a lot of people out there who aren't fond of camping, but I am not one of them. I love to camp, and I'm okay with rustic. Turns out the Kiwis are fond of camping, too, and Jim and I benefited mightily from the result: there were oodles of campgrounds—most towns had one—and all were welcoming with great amenities. We found this out on our first night in Picton at the Top 10 Holiday Park.

"Pitch your tent wherever you want," said the cheerful young woman at check-in. We stopped in front of a hedge- and tree-bordered grassy slope next to a gurgling creek. There were already several small tents on the grass. Jim insisted on a mostly isolated spot, up against hedges.

Kiwi campgrounds are different from the American version; few have numbered sites, although some have separate areas for motor vehicles versus tents. They also have large kitchens to be a shared by all, first-come, first-served, with stoves, fridges, tables, pots, pans, utensils, even TVs—you name it. And while they don't have picnic tables, they do usually have an outdoor, communal picnic area with gas-powered barbecues. At mealtimes, the camp kitchens turned into bustling, festive places. I headed over to cook dinner our first night. Jim, by far a better cook than I, usually did dinner, but he was loath to cook in such a public place.

"No, I'm not going over there to cook," he insisted. "And I'm still tuning the bikes."

"But there are no picnic tables here," I steamed, exasperated with his antisocial pigheadedness.

"Whaddya gonna do, start up the one-burner in the grass? Think how stupid that is when there is a fully outfitted kitchen."

"I don't care," he replied. "I'm still tuning the bikes. You cook tonight."

"Okay," I said. "I'll cook in the kitchen but I am NOT bringing the food back here. If you want to eat with me, make your way over in twenty minutes or so with our plates and silverware." A small victory, but I knew he was hungry enough that he would have to give in.

As I cooked, the kitchen turned into a United Nations of Happy Campers, getting busier and busier. Everyone came with libations, mostly wine or beer. The cooking was not just in the kitchen; there was also an outdoor barbecue with multiple grills and picnic tables. The party was on, and I loved it. I chose to lay low until someone talked to me. Every night was a surprise—I never knew who I was going to meet. Once the Kiwis knew I was American, I got a lot of tips on cycling, camping . . . well, all things adventurous. Jim finally let go of his natural reticence and joined me, though it was not his favorite part of the day.

Returning to our tent after our first dinner, we met Heidi, a young Swiss woman who had biked a month on the North Island and had double that for the South. She tipped us off to the extensive shuttle bus network. Designed for Kiwi backpackers heading to remote mountain trails, anyone could make a reservation. She told us she used the shuttles to get past the places she didn't like or with too much traffic. Thanks to her, we ended up taking four shuttles to get around the trafficked and windy parts of the island.

Keen to get an early start the next morning, I was the first one in the camp kitchen. I wanted to make coffee, oatmeal, and soup for the thermos. After setting water to boil in not one, not two, but three small, beat-up pots, I laid out a map to study our options for the day. As I sat there, a youngish athletic man came in, nodded, looked at me quizzically and walked over to this big aluminum box attached to the wall above one of the counters. He pulled a little black lever and out poured steaming—and I mean *steaming*—hot water straight into his big plastic mug. Then he turned and walked out. Huh? I went over to the box and pulled the lever—oops. Steaming hot water splashed on the counter. I slinked on over to the stove, turned off the burners, dumped the water into the sink and headed on over to this thing of wonder—instant hot water on demand. Such a thing I had never seen in my forty-nine years of existence, but as a lover of blazingly hot coffee, I was totally twitter-pated. Almost every campground we stayed at had one of these marvelous devices in their camp kitchens, and each day on the bikes, I'd dream about the hot cup of coffee or tea awaiting me.

Our second night, we met eight Scottish men on a tour that included not only rented Harley Davidsons, but a Kiwi woman who drove a sag wagon—a fully equipped vehicle providing all necessary support and cooked two meals a day for the group—talk about posh.

The daily encounters in the camp kitchens was one of the many things that really made this trip for me. I loved to compare notes and equipment. We found the Kiwis open, comfortable, friendly in a polite sort of not-pushy way, and athletic as all hell. Over and over again, they welcomed us, helped us out, and gave us good tips for the road ahead.

At the Riverton campground, we met John, a retired Brit who pulled in on his bike just after us and set up his tent close to us. He was one year into a three-year world international cycling tour. At age fifty-six, he raced bikes in England before he retired and decided to travel the world. For the next six days, we leap-frogged one another during the day; he passed us when we stopped for lunch on the way up Haast Pass; we passed him when he stopped for

Chapter 17

takeaway. We saw each other climbing Fox Glacier, taking the same day off the bikes, and each night, we found each other in the same campground. Jim came to look forward to it—he was keen to learn as much as he could from John who he saw as much more experienced. John's stories from his year on the road inspired Jim to wonder if we could do it, too.

After a week of cycling, on a soaking, rainy day, we pulled into a campground and I noticed a semicircle of six brightly painted huts.

"What are those cute, bright huts for?" I asked the older woman who checked us in.

"Oh, those are overnight rentals, bare-bones inside, pretty minimal. They're popular with backpackers who just carry flimsy tents. Gives them more room before they head into the mountains."

"Wow, I had no idea. How much for a night?"

"Five dollars more than tent camping, but there's nothing inside but two metal cots and a ceiling light. And only the turquoise one is still available. You want it?"

"Sure. Better than pitching our tent in the rain," I couldn't wait to get out to share this with Jim. Three more times, we arrived at campgrounds in the rain and took advantage of a hut—a godsend to pile into and not have to pitch a tent in the rain. What was not to love about cycling New Zealand?

I totally fell for the style of Kiwi campgrounds, their big expanses of Bermuda grass lawns that gradually filled up, higgledy-piggledy in the course of the evening—with RVs, campers, vans, tents, cars, bikes, and motorbikes—first-come first-served. No designated campsites here. And the vans cracked me up—I came to call them Barbie vans because they were so tiny (by American standards), they seemed better suited for dolls than people. Most Barbie vans were white, stripped-down shells. These mini vans were ubiquitous, making camping and nature affordable to those willing to sacrifice space for convenience.

One morning, as I walked to the kitchen, a man over six feet tall extricated himself from a Barbie van that was shorter than he was long. The whiz of the door caught my attention. I turned and watched him grab the door jamb with both hands and swing out like a gymnast. Later, in the kitchen, he told me he was American, from Anaheim, and was circling the island by himself. Two weeks was all he could afford, but preferred the van to a tent.

We didn't just stay in campgrounds, though. Twice, we spent the night in farm-stays, and they couldn't have been more different. The Staging Post in Hawksdown was a dilapidated farm that felt straight out of the nineteenth century.

Run by Abigail, the place was quite shabby and funky. She suggested a log cabin with crumpled newspapers in the cracks, a floor of hard-packed dirt, and in the middle of the room was a two-foot-wide, one-foot-high tree stump. There was an unheated pool, which we promptly jumped in and just as promptly jumped out, heading to much preferable heated showers. We were on our own for dinner, but found a small carton of cold milk outside our door the next morning.

Our second farm-stay, at Shirley and Colin's farm in Otara at the southernmost part of the island, couldn't have been more different. It was an immaculate, comfortable, well-run, and efficient, modern farm. The Staging Post cabin cost $10 a night; Shirley and Colin's cost $100.

Chapter 17

When Shirley gave us her hour-long tour of the farm, she talked about "flares." I didn't have a clue what she was talking about until she pointed to a flower. I caught her again during dinner when she referred to her son "A-van"—for Evan. She let me do our wash on the condition I hung it up myself, for they had no dryer.

Pointing to the back door, she said, "The clothesline is out that door. If you ignore the rams, they'll ignore you." Jim was napping, Shirley was cooking dinner, and Colin was out and about somewhere on the farm when I carried everything, except for the outfits we wore, out the back door. I paused, caught my breath, and almost turned right around—there were sixteen rams, and each one looked like they weighed about the same as me. But she was right; the rams were too busy shaving down the penned-in lawn to pay me any attention. At dinner, Shirley said it was a "sight to see" when they let the sixteen rams loose in the field with their 1,200 ewes.

Besides farm-stays, there were lots of budget accommodations. Less fancy than American B&Bs, many guesthouses and hostels include communal kitchens, like the campgrounds. An older German woman ran a guesthouse in Milton, but when I tried to book a room with her, she wasn't comfortable speaking English. I knew no German, so we switched to French.

On one of our last days, we pulled into the town of Takaka and decided to splurge on a guesthouse for two nights so we could ride the thirty-five miles, unloaded, to Wharariki Beach. Tani and Kath ran a backpacker establishment, and although it had a communal kitchen, the rest was really bare-bones. Older than us, and Kath being from Oregon, I inquired about a private room. She said they had an empty bedroom in their house next door that they sometimes let out.

For a little bit more, we got to sleep two nights in a scrumptious bed with linens and an en suite bathroom with a triangle-shaped tub that fit us both. We had time to explore the cute-as-a-button downtown and got booted out of a gift shop that specialized in hand-turned native wood dishes. Jim and I were both struck by a beautiful $35 bowl, but we had misgivings about carrying it. Before we could decide, the clerk told us it was closing time and asked us to leave.

After loading up on hot tea and delicious pastries the next day, we flew thirty-five miles north on a gloriously sunny day to a long peninsular spit with a pale gray, soft-as-silk sandy beach. The beach is as close as Jim comes to religion. We were nearing the end of our trip and he was feeling playful.

"We shoulda bought that bowl last night, it was beautiful. And only $35 Kiwi dollars."

"Yeah, we didn't have time before closing."

"How far are we? What time is it? Maybe we can get back before five?"

"Oh, we're thirty-five miles away, Jim. No way, it's just past two."

"Let's try," he replied. "Pack up, quick."

We raced, urging each other on, up and over the five uppies and pulled into town with ten minutes to spare, enough time for me to go inside and buy it while Jim guarded the bikes. A shiny, deep-brown and yellow golden bowl, 11" wide and 4" deep, shaped and polished out of a silver beech burl. The pattern resembles bird's-eye maple; circular curlicues with edges that retain the rough-edged burl. Jim lovingly carried it the remaining days, and it sits on the table near me as I write.

Chapter 17

There were so many wonderful surprises to New Zealand. One of the best, though, was the food. As we biked south of Dunedin, we crested a hill, and there on the side of the road was a camper trailer with a big blue and white sign: Fish and Chips. I looked back at Jim and he yelled "Yes!" without my saying a word. The trailer, with big blue and white striped awning, had a hand-written chalkboard sign out front listing the fish of the day. We propped our bikes up against one of two picnic tables and walked over to check out our choices.

"*Kia ora,*" said the young man from inside. "What'll ya have?" Now, it's true that anything tastes better after riding for a few hours, but the fresh blue cod just melted in our mouths—Jim liked it so much he went back and ordered a second serving. We must of stopped at a half dozen fish shacks, usually close to the coast, but in the middle of nowhere. It just made a day to stumble on such a simple and delicious food option.

Another great surprise in the food department was Kiwi tea salons. First off, let me say the Kiwis are serious about their hot water—every campground had hot, hot water in their kitchens and bathrooms (though not usually their swimming pools), hot enough to burn, so I learned to be careful. Same was true of coffee and tea. I so hate going into an American restaurant and getting a tepid cup of tea that I rarely order it. However, when one orders a pot of tea in New Zealand, it comes blazingly hot, and most places include a full refill in the price. Then, add to this the Kiwi talent for making great pastries, especially scones. For me, it was a match made in heaven. Tea salons abounded in the towns of the South Island, and each morning as we pedaled I wondered, *Where's the next one gonna be?*

***

Two days south of Dunedin, we entered an isolated, rugged landscape where the road deteriorated in quality. Steeper than average slopes appeared, asphalt disappeared into washboarded dirt—sometimes encountering one, sometimes the other, and sometimes both. Then the going got rough. While I'd developed thunder thighs as a result of all our cycling over the years, I easily lost my confidence when I needed to throw in all my upper body strength. We were still ten miles from day's end, Papatowai Campground, following the bucolic Catlins River as far as we could, and the ozone-depleted sun was bearing down on us. Now, the steepest slope of the trip appeared before me. It looked about a 15 percent grade and I bonked, worried if I could stay upright with the hot sun beating down. Jim knew I was uncertain and tried to reassure me.

"You can do it. Let's stop and rest—have a drink."

I looked up the steep slope. It was so hot. "I don't know, maybe I should just walk it." Just then, a beat-up white pickup with thin black, silver, and red stripes and a camper shell slowed down and pulled over in front of us. Two scrawny little numbers got out, and the older one spoke.

"Greetings. Wanna lift up the hill?"

"Oh, yes," I immediately piped up. And then I turned to Jim, and the look on his face—the disappointment. He didn't say a word, though. I think he was stunned into silence.

The younger one opened the back of the truck. It was half filled with fishing and camping gear.

"Looks like there's not enough room," Jim spoke up quickly, thrilled to be thwarted. "Thanks for the offer."

The older guy was chagrined, "Sorry mate. I forgot how much stuff we have. Is there anything else we can do?"

Jim smiled and said, "Just a cold beer." We all laughed. They both shook hands with Jim, tipped their hats to me, and climbed in their truck. I was a little disappointed, but tried not to show it as I picked up my bike.

Jim breathed a sigh of relief, "We can do this, you can do this Anne. Just take it nice and slow." So I mounted my bike, stayed upright, and kept going. Thankfully, the steepest grade was the first part; once past that, I was fine.

Jim yelled out from behind, "Let's stop at the top for another rest."

"Okay," I said, although I thought he was babying me. Thirty minutes later as we approached the summit I saw a pickup ahead on a turnout. As I noticed it had stripes, Jim called out, "Is that their truck?"

And, sure enough, as we got closer, we saw they were standing at the back with the tailgate open. The older one flew open the lid of a cooler, and pulled out four icy bottles of beer.

"Here ya go, mate."

Jim and I looked at each other, then back at them, and we all started laughing. "We thought you'd enjoy it more at the top of the hill than the bottom," the older one said.

"I meant it as a joke, but I'd love one," Jim replied.

"Me, too," I exclaimed, still astounded by the surprise.

"I'm Mark," he said. "I'm 'Straylan [Australian]; came over forty years ago to shear sheep and stayed. This is Bill, my son, born here, so unfortunately, he's a Kiwi," he laughed.

"We're on holiday," volunteered Bill. "We're going to spend the week fishing and drinking, so we're not in any rush, and we've got a lot of brew."

The cold beers went down fast. Again we thanked them, and Mark and Bill sped away.

"That's Down Under hospitality," I said. "What you made as a crack, he took as a mandate."

"Yeah, part of me feels bad they had to wait so long for us to reach them on the summit, but their beer sure hit the spot."

As the days turned into weeks, I came to realize another reason why it was so much fun to bike the South Island: pretty much except for the stretch on the east coast from Christchurch to Dunedin (which we chose not to bike but to bus), there are no freeways. You could say, and I will, the South Island is a pre-1950s landscape, that is, a place where towns were built on an assumption that many people still live and work within walking distance of the basic amenities. When we pedaled into town, we almost always found a campground within walking distance of not just our Big Three (grocery stores, restaurants and libraries), but *all* the services a town offers—shoe repair, pharmacies, bookstores, hardware, etc. Walking distance. No big deal to those in a car, RV, or camping van, but a big deal for us. To spend four to six hours pedaling up and down hills, against the wind, sometimes on dirt roads, and then be able to enjoy a town on foot just made every day fun.

That's another thing I came to realize about myself as a result of our unorthodox form of travel: I can bite off a lot. I'm willing to push my body hard for the ride, but it's so much easier to keep going when there is a payoff, a new delight, each day. With each successive challenge and experience, Jim and I came to learn what we were made of. The days we were tested, the pain was easier to tolerate when there was a reward at the end of the day, and made it easier to get back in the saddle the next day, wondering what that day's surprise might be

Although I had no idea before we got here, Jim really nailed it when he chose New Zealand for our first big adventure, and it didn't take long for us to realize Rushton really knew what he was talking about—the South Island of New Zealand was truly a pedaler's paradise for us. New Zealand is full of incredibly athletic people who love to take advantage of the diverse landscape by engaging in all forms of sporty tourism, hiking and backpacking the vast, remote Fiordland. This meant the demand was so high there were all sorts of reasonably priced amenities for energetic tourists: great campgrounds, a nimble, easily accessible shuttle system, delicious, reasonably priced food and drink, and the best roads for cycling of any place we had pedaled so far. We returned home more enthused and confident than ever. We traveled well together and were able to have a good time because our strengths complimented each other. While many thought we were foolish to travel as a unsupported twosome, we discovered another lesson, #22: We Make a Pretty Good Team.

Fox Mountain and what's left of its glacier

Enjoying a beer with Aussie Mark and his Kiwi son Bill

View of Picton harbor from the ferry

Taking a break on Lake Hawea

EIGHTEEN

Beyond California #2: Following the Hot Water

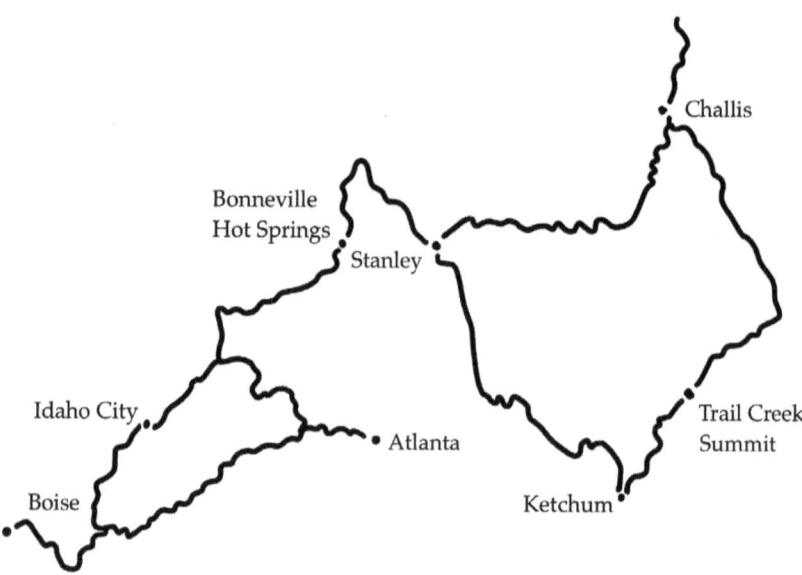

Our daughter, Eleanor, drove us to SFO for a second bike tour via plane—this time, sixteen days in Idaho, continuing our preferred style of travel: a start and stop time and place; the rest to be decided. We would head northeast from Boise and see how far we would get before we had to turn around.

We both liked traveling loosey-goosey, but I still needed maps; I thrived on them, and loved when I found a guidebook that included maps. My primary source for this trip was *Hot Springs of the Pacific Northwest*, recommended by a co-worker of Jim's when we told him we were going to bike Idaho. It had good details and easy-to-follow maps, so once again, we'd be following the water, but instead of cold rivers, we'd be chasing down hot springs.

I booked the earliest flight possible so we'd have time to assemble the bikes at the airport, buy supplies, and pedal twenty miles to a campground. After the debacle in New Zealand lugging bikes in sacks, I was determined not to repeat that mistake. We found a quiet corner in the Boise airport parking lot and assembled both bikes in just under three hours—a full hour less than last time. It was delicious to just pedal away from the airport, skirting the city to the south and picking up the Boise River to the northeast. I felt like we had won the lottery.

We stopped to get groceries and cooking fuel. Soon after, the suburbs gave way and we began a slow and gradual climb to Lucky Peak Dam and the 3,782-foot Highland Valley Summit. Lots of scarps, dramatic vertical rock formations, kept us entertained as we pedaled. Then, at the summit, we spied a restaurant. The hell with cooking tonight, we'd enjoy what the chefs at Hilltop Station offered. No surprise, it had a Western theme and was mostly empty when we waltzed in at 4:30 p.m. We both opted for a traditional dinner because they came with potatoes, figuring when in Rome, do as the Romans. We looked forward to sampling Idaho potatoes—until our first bite. They had the chutzpah to serve us processed mashed potatoes. Yuck, I refused to eat them.

Three miles past the peak, Jim spied out a beautiful place to free-camp on the Boise River with a great view, a sandy beach, and a grove of poplar trees to hide our tent. We were going to bike another six miles to a bona fide campground, but this spot was so pretty and we were mighty tired; it'd been fourteen hours since our alarm went off at 4 a.m. The river was warm enough to swim, wiping off all the day's sweat and toil as we enjoyed our own private campground.

In the morning, we picked up a dirt road along Middle Fork of the Boise River. The guidebook showed many hot springs all the way to the old mining town of Atlanta. Idaho would not disappoint; in sixteen days we ended up soaking twenty-one times in eleven different hot springs. Four we found along the road, and seven at campgrounds that either had a hot spring or one near enough to walk to. We found them in every imaginable setting. Some were along the banks of rivers, one was in the river; we could see it bubbling up, generating steam in the swiftly flowing cold water, only becoming accessible later summer when the water level dropped. Sometimes we had to hike up cliffs, down overgrown paths, or around marshes. In the old mining town of Atlanta, we learned the hot spring in a stand of trees a ways out of town was actually the de facto town bathing facility. Lois, the owner of the Beaver Lodge, told us the town now had only thirty-five residents, and most had no running water in their homes. As a result, the Atlanta hot springs had a unique protocol: Only one group in at a time, it's okay to bathe with soap but the pool must be drained and cleaned before departure. Others arriving must wait at a discreet distance to ensure privacy.

We learned that the protocol for the primitive ones along the side of the road is the new arrival should ask those already in the water if it is okay if they join them, if they were comfortable with clothing optional. Many were locally built and maintained, with the water contained inside rocks and boulders, logs and beams, sometimes held together with concrete. The last one, along the Payette River, had a round, slatted wood hot tub installed, with a bucket attached by a rope. The bucket was essential—the spring water so hot we had to add a dozen buckets of river water before we could get in.

Oh, the hot springs were a wonderful treat each day, all out in nature and wild. Sometimes we'd find them early in the day and Jim wouldn't want to stop, but there was no way I was passing up the opportunity to soak. Some had sandy bottoms that you could squish your toes in while soaking. Some were a bit too hot, some a bit too cool, but all were great on the bod and the muscles no matter the setting or how early it was; a refreshing break that made it easier to get back in the saddle.

At the first hot spring, we could see the steam from the road. It was a short way up an easy slope, a big, rock-framed semicircle cemented in place with the hot water dripping down into the pool. As we undressed, we realized there was yet another pool ten feet or so above this one, again ringed in by cemented stones, both with sandy bottoms. Another couple, locals, showed up in a beat-up pickup as we were getting ready to leave. They came pretty regularly and told us that Atlanta had two great hot springs. We thanked them and took off. Bumping along, we wondered about the wisdom of taking on a hundred miles of washboarded dirt road, but the hot springs were so enticing. The real challenge came when we realized Atlanta was seventeen miles down a dead-end road. The recommendations were too great to pass up.

We spent a lot of time on dirt roads, many in pretty bad shape, often rutted and washboarded. The seventeen miles to Atlanta was about the worst. Jim regretted not getting new tires. So far, he'd had three flats, one each day, and he realized his patch kit was getting low on patches. We were dusty and hungry when we pulled into town and found there were only two open businesses—both were bars. The 2000 Trail Creek fire had decimated 33,000 acres, coming right up to the edge of the town, but still the town was in pretty bad shape.

Jim wanted to check out each before deciding. We sensed a real division between the two, one was an old-time, family kind of place with beer on tap. The other seemed run by liberal hippy types and only sold beer in bottles. The beer on tap settled it for us. Lois, the owner, made us welcome. Her daughter-in-law, Kathy, waited our table and we got Mosquitoed by their neighbor Charlene who sat at the bar. About fifty, I'd guess, skinny arms and legs with a tummy that said she liked her beer.

"Where are you from?"

Jim rolled his eyes so I replied, "The Bay Area. We flew in two days ago."

"You biked here? From Boise?" she exclaimed. "Whadda you, crazy?"

"Yeah, that's what they say," Jim replied.

Kathy brought our burgers, fries, and beer on tap, "Let 'em eat in peace, Charlene."

"But I gotta know where they're going. Where are you going?" she laughed as she eyed Kathy that she wasn't ready to stop.

"We don't know, for sure," I answered. "We came here because we're following the hot springs. We've got sixteen days. This is day three."

"It's eighty-five miles to Boise," Charlene volunteered. "That's mighty slow going. Why didn't you just rent a car?"

"We can't afford the gas," Jim piped up. "Plus, with a car, we'd have to stay in hotels. With the bikes, we can free-camp."

"Now we've got questions for you three," I said and peppered them with questions in between bites about the springs, the town, living in a remote, rugged place like Atlanta, the roads, the campgrounds. I eat faster than Jim, so we finished about the same time, and I got lots of helpful info. Instead of desert, Jim and I each ordered a second beer on tap. Lois informed us about the town hot spring, its rules, and that it was on the way to the campground. When we went past, there was no one in it, so we postponed setting up camp to enjoy a soak. It was so lovely we went again later that night and a third time in the morning on our way out of town.

We skipped cooking breakfast in camp the next morning, opting to eat at Lois's bar. After we ordered, I asked Kathy if we could buy some burgers, buns, cheese, and eggs to go. There was no grocery store for miles upon miles, but she had a great stock of fresh food and it was a real kindness of her to sell it to us—at cost, no less. It meant that night we got to eat a yummy, fresh dinner after another hard day on dirt roads. Finally, on day four, after about 120 miles of dirt and four flat tires, we returned to glorious asphalt. It never fails; after riding on dirt roads, getting back to asphalt feels like a hot knife through butter. We had to climb to 6,000 feet, though, so by the time we got to that night's campground, Bonneville, we were really looking forward to soaking in the adjacent hot springs. Trouble was, when we got there the sign said closed.

"Let's go," Jim immediately said. "We can find something up the road."

"No," I insisted. "The tourist board in Lowman said this place was open," I pedaled in and Jim reluctantly followed me. We passed a construction crew laying new asphalt, and when we arrived at the campground host, there were two women sitting outside.

"Hey," the older one said, "this campground is closed."

"Oh, but," I replied sweetly, "we checked in at the tourist office in Lowman and they told us you were open. So we biked forty-six miles to get here." The older women, white haired, rugged in jeans and cowboy boots, sighed, scratched her head and glared at the younger woman.

"I thought I told you to call Lowman?"

"I forgot," The younger woman exclaimed. It was easy to guess she was her daughter, so similar but no gray hair yet.

Quickly, I piped up, "It's just two of us on bikes, no car. We can easily stay out of the way of the crew, and if you'll let us stay, we promise to leave in the morning before they even start up. We easily went around them today. And we're so tired." I eventually wore the old lady down.

"Okay, that was our bad. If you promise to stay out of the crew's way, I guess you can camp back there with no one else the wiser. Make sure you're gone before seven. And while you're back there, enjoy the hot springs—you'll have them to yourself tonight. And once the crew is done, the road will be gated to keep cars off their work." I looked at Jim and beamed, and he gave me that look that meant he knew there was no use resisting me. Oh, it was a great night. We were unable to buy any fresh food that day, so the meals were pretty bland, but who cared about eating when we had the hot springs to ourselves?

The Bonneville Hot Springs was different yet again. We climbed up a slope from the campground to an enormous, grassy field that had a rushing, cold-water, sandy-bottom stream racing through the middle of it; some parts constrained in a narrow channel, others widening out and turning into a swampy marsh. And in various spots, steam rose from the cold water. Wherever there was a spring, there was some type of man-made construction to fashion a catch basin for the hot water to mix with the cold stream. It was a tricky business finding spots with an ideal temperature. The guidebook said the unadulterated hot water came out at 185 degrees, while the creek was in the fifties. Some of the marshy parts were thick with moss. We went back and forth, flitting from pool to pool, chasing the perfect spot. Then, while sitting in one, I noticed a hut fifty feet up a steep slope, with pipes leading in and out of it. Curious, I wrapped myself in a towel, put on my shoes, hiked up, and opened the rough-wood creaking door. There was a stained, clawfoot bathtub with two spigots pouring in, and one draining out. I tested the temperature; 100 degrees or a bit more. I took off my shoes, hung my towel on one of the handmade hooks, opened the door, and yelled down to Jim.

"Come on up," Back in I went, just bliss! I got up before sunrise the next day to get in another soak.

In the cool morning air, we climbed 2,500 feet in fifteen miles to Banner Summit—7,200 feet. Then we coasted the next twenty-five miles through dense, quiet forest to the town of Stanley. Just short of town, Jim got his fifth flat tire of the trip and used his second-to-last patch.

"We've gotta get new tubes and a patch kit in this town, or we might not be able to continue," he fumed as he fixed his flat. We were happily surprised to find a bustling town; as we encountered so few people, we began to wonder if Idahoans had discovered s-e-x yet. Stanley sat at the intersection of three roads that lead to all sorts of outdoor mountain activities, so it had a lot to offer us. Not only multiple restaurants and grocery stores, but a library and, thankfully, sporting goods stores. Only the main highway through town was paved, all the other streets were dirt. In the sporting goods store, Jim mentioned our plan to bike over Summit Peak but the clerk urged us not to do it.

"Oh, I don't think that's a good idea for bicycles," he said. "The road is pretty rough; no pavement and lots of boulders. Plus, it's popular with the off-road vehicle crowd, and I'm not sure those guys will give you the time of day."

When we stopped to fill up on a cooked meal at Roosevelt's Bar and Grill the next day in Ketchum, we chatted with our twenty-something waiter and told him we planned to climb Summit Peak. He too thought we were crazy.

"No way you're gonna make it up and over, the Summit Peak Road is too rough for bicycles." But we were in a pickle, or I was more than Jim, if we *didn't* take that road; we'd have to retrace our steps, no loop. I picked Summit Peak Road to do a loop. Their negative reaction reminded us of the reaction of the motorcyclists in San Benito County, roads that aren't doable for motorists certainly can be for cyclists. Dirt and rocks aren't a problem if they're hard-packed. It's the soft stuff we can't manage, like in Death Valley, or a grade so steep I have to walk. Plus, all the naysayers got us up on our hind legs.

"Let's go for it," Jim said. "We'll show them." Another chance to try lesson #20.

"Well," I replied, "they won't be around, but we can prove it to ourselves. And if it is too hard, we'll just turn around. Just like in San Benito County. But we made it there."

We left the much-too-touristed Ketchum and climbed a narrow valley with steep hills covered with brush lower down, pine trees toward the top and snow strung out along the summit. The grade stayed manageable and the road was hard-packed dirt. It's true, there were lots of sections of degraded surfaces, boulders, and puddles, but we plodded along on a slow but steady climb to 7,950 feet, proving all the cynics wrong. And we saw only four trucks the entire two-hour climb, no off-roaders, maybe because it was a Thursday.

At the summit, there was a great wooded campground, Park Creek, but it was too early to stop. On the descent, we were framed in by a lovely forest with snow-capped mountains all around. We stopped at a wooded spot along a creek with a soft, grass-covered island, pushed our bikes over a log bridge, and set up camp. Next morning, Jim made out what he guessed were moose prints in the dirt under our tied-up dry sack, and in two lines, crossing the island and right through the bare patch where we cooked the night before, just feet from our tent. As we pedaled away, we were glad they didn't hassle us.

***

I need to mention the incredible variety and condition of the log cabins everywhere—there were several on the route from Chilly to Challis. They came in all possible shapes and sizes and ages. Some were tiny and some half-buried in the ground. Many of the older ones were in an advanced state of decay and collapse. These often were located adjacent to newer homes on the farms, where maybe the grandparents or great-grandparents who settled the place started. Then, with time and prosperity, a better home was built. People here were still building log cabin homes, some quite simple and low-cost, others quite grandiose.

It was a great to pull into the Challis campground, with a hot-springs-fed 90-degree large pool with a pebble-rock bottom and a smaller, hotter pool. I just loved that there were two pools of different temperatures—it's great for the muscles to go back and forth. By late afternoon, the place filled up with Baby Boomers on motorcycles. Most were fatter and older than us, all were on huge bikes, and more than half pulled mini RVs. It turned into quite the evening; a full-on party time for what we learned is an annual convention for this Harley group from Boise. The big pool was full all evening with these gray-haired bikers, though most avoided the hot pool. Just as well, many of them had plastic containers with contraband liquids, I presume.

Unfortunately, the town of Challis was three miles away as the crow flies, but nine miles by bike. I was much too tired after our first soak to climb back on my bike, but I knew Jim was eager enough for liquid replenishments that he would go without me. He wanted to get away from the bedlam while I relished sticking around and watching the action. I was surprised how spacious some very compact trailers became when opened up. I would have loved to have seen the inside of a few.

Jim came back with the makings for fresh dinner, another nice bottle of local wine, and good news.

"There's a mercantile store in town. I want to go tomorrow and check out the clothes, but it doesn't open until ten. Let's get a lazy start, okay?" It didn't take much to convince me; I'd have more time for soaking and people-watching.

In the morning, we opted to skip cooking and stopped in town for breakfast at a roadhouse recommended by the campground host. It was a Saturday morning and the place was hoppin' with locals, young and old, families with kids, a table with single men sipping coffee. Many chatted across tables with the people they knew, catching up on town news. A lot of the men were in full cowboy attire—jeans, flannel shirts with snaps, and cowboy boots. Some of them were in what I called half cowboy mode—jeans and boots but T-shirts and baseball caps.

We had San Benito and New Zealand to thank for our newfound willingness to go into more bars on this trip. I was never a bar person; even during my dating years they made me uneasy. But, really, it made perfect sense when we passed one in the hot afternoon. I became fascinated by the architecture, both animate and inanimate, in mostly fleabag country bars. The signs, paraphernalia, neon lights, etc., were often irreverent and bawdy. The Dusty Mule at Elk Bend offered beer in cups in the shape of boobs and dicks—at no extra cost, you just had to ask. The Rocks Bar near Idaho City had a counter laminated with pages from an old Sears Roebuck catalog. The locals and bartenders were an unpredictable lot, too, colorful and often defiant. The locals often looked at us askance when we first entered in our unorthodox garb, but by the time we had a beer or two, they accepted us as part of The Drinking Tribe, so we were tolerated—for a little while. We never stayed long, but we left with memories of a lot of colorful characters, sometimes the reticent bartenders, but more often the bar flies.

We hadn't realized how far and how long we had really been from civilization until we pulled into Idaho City the day before our departure. Jim surprised me by stopping in front of a laundromat.

"I stink, and all my clothes do, too," he said. "I don't want to get on the plane this dirty. How about we do a batch of wash? If you do the wash, I'll shop for dinner and cook tonight." As much as I hated to admit he was right, I didn't want to waste time in a laundromat (I would have hand-washed two outfits in the river that night). But I didn't argue. Idaho City was a beat-up, working class, former boom town with a lot of rundown buildings and mobile homes in even worse shape, the kind of place that may have a "Gateway To . . ." sign as you pull into town. Lesson #23: Beware of a Gateway To Sign at the Entrance of a Town; it's a pretty sure bet the place is a shithole just on the border of Someplace Famous cashing in on its proximity.

After packing up our freshly washed clothes, we tanked up at Trudy's Kitchen. The place had all kinds of vintage kitchen appliances and tools on the walls.

"Hey," Jim exclaimed, "there's huckleberry cheesecake on the menu." We shared a slice for dessert and it was delicious—creamy, purple-magenta with whipping cream. It really was the cherry-on-top ending to our trip. Then, back in the saddle for a slick twenty-two-mile descent along Mores

Creek to free-camp in the same spot as our first night, along the banks of the Boise River.

As we set up camp, scores of Canada geese flew past us, landing on the water. Then a boat pulling two big orange-ball buoys headed out into the water laying ropes as it went—it looked like there was going to be a race of some sort. On our ride down the next morning, we saw the setup for a triathlon, with bikes stationed in the parking lot waiting for their riders. We got all the way into town without catching a glimpse of the event. I guess we were too early.

We found Boise bustling, the annual summer festival was just getting started, and we had a couple of hours before we had to head to the airport. So we picked a coffee shop with outdoor seating on a busy corner and settled in to watch the show. Quite a few people found us to be the show, stopping to ask about our loaded bikes. The people in Idaho, like the Kiwis on the previous trip, were incredibly friendly. Maybe it had something to do with how few of them there are. Idaho was so sparsely populated, it made the riding a lot less stressful. Idaho was vast, mountainous—we climbed seven summits in sixteen days. It was dry, Western, lots of log cabins of every size, shape, and condition. In Ketchum, we saw cabins big enough to fit ten of the dilapidated numbers in them, with shiny, deep-red logs a foot in diameter, more like palaces. I liked the beat-up ones better; split wood, cracked windows, holes in the walls the size of wheelbarrows. I wondered if some dated from the nineteenth century. Back in the twenty-first, we bid adieu to cheery Boise, made our way to the airport, and broke apart the bikes in one hour, thirty minutes.

Another trip finished, and again another learning experience. The more we rode, the more we loved getting to know the places we traveled. We knew, for example, we'd be following the hot water, but falling in love with log cabins and well-worn bars were added delights. And the people-watching—in the campgrounds, the restaurants, towns—again, we went home happy campers.

Sawtooth Mountains

Assembling the bikes at Boise airport

Shack in Sawtooth Valley

NINETEEN

Beyond California #3: Snow & Ice

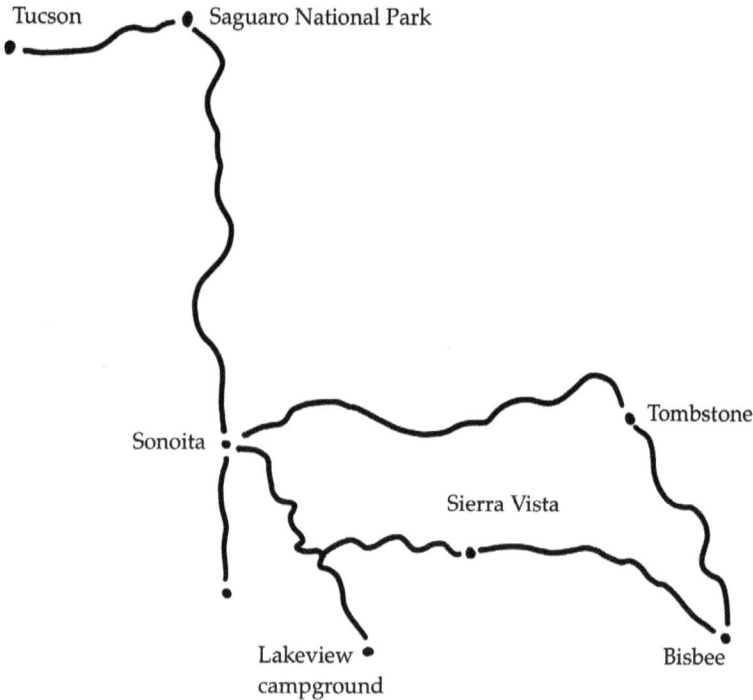

"How about Arizona for your winter break this year?" Jim suggested on the way home from Thanksgiving dinner in San Carlos. "With the couplings, we could fly instead of drive."

"Won't it be too cold?" I asked.

"Look on the map. There's a couple of big deserts, like Death Valley and the Mohave. We managed Death Valley in January, why not Arizona? We can spend the first night in a hotel, I can assemble the bikes in our room. And if we book the same place on the way back, we can wash our clothes and be clean for the flight home, like in Boise." He turned and gave me a look.

"You know, I planned to wash our clothes when we swam in the Boise River that night, instead of hanging in that laundromat for three hours. I'd much rather have done it myself and had more time to relax at the campsite."

"Anne, you're too thrifty, live a little. It was great having clean clothes on the plane. And it's lots easier to spend the first and last nights in a hotel room. Remember how nice it was in Buellton?"

After exploring the maps, I carved out a loop. We settled on flying into Tucson and heading towards the Chihuahuan Desert to the south. A friend of ours told us about the eclectic town of Bisbee, about a hundred miles from Tucson; I fashioned a loop mostly on back roads.

Four weeks later, complimentary New Year's Eve champagne put everyone on our plane in a festive mood, although I sobered up fast looking out the window as we landed—the Tucson Mountains were so close us I thought they might scrape the plane's wheels off. Then we had several abrupt jolts of turbulence that sent a few unstrapped passengers tumbling. Were these warning signs?

As Jim laid out the bike parts on the floor of our hotel room, he discovered a broken spoke on his back wheel.

"I can't carry all my gear with a missing back spoke. I should have packed backups. Next trip, I will, for sure. Look up the closest bike shop, and if we can get to one before dinner, I can replace the spoke before we take off in the morning."

"The closest one is four miles away, Tucson is huge." I said as the TV announced the weather forecast: three days of sunshine, and then three days of rain.

"Sounds good," Jim said. "We could get camping fuel, too."

Next morning on the road to Saguaro Park, we passed a German bakery, Schlotzsky's, so we stopped for a loaf of bread. Boy, did they have some great stuff in there. We must have pedaled about fifteen miles before we finally got to Saguaro National Park on the eastern side of town. There's a popular eight-mile, one-way loop through a high-desert landscape of browns, reds, and yellows, with hundreds of saguaros sharing the landscape with many other lesser known types of cacti. Saguaros live about 200 years and don't grow arms until they're seventy-five.

Besides a few birds the only wildlife we saw was a rabbit. It didn't run away and I managed to take a picture of it through the bushes. It was very thin with spindly legs. There were a lot of cyclists. Because of our gear, some slowed to talk to a few; a couple who biked eleven months in Australia and a woman who did the 1976 Centennial Across America Ride. An Aussie couple gave me their Tucson phone number—if we needed emergency help, just call, they said.

Chapter 19

After filling up on the hotel breakfast, we headed southeast without even thinking about eating, passing up two restaurants and a corner store. But once we were good and out in the middle of nowhere, I bonked. I suddenly got ravenously hungry, started feeling woozy. Anxiety and doubt set in. Jim knew me well enough to read the signs.

"That's enough," Jim said. "And this looks as good a place as any to spend the night." So we set up the tent in a lovely little valley with grass, cacti, bushes . . . hiding is fun. Our site was really terrific. We had mountain ridges all around, but were sheltered and alone in a serene setting. Off in the distance, several times in the night, coyotes started a raucous chorus, building to a fevered pitch before tapering off.

The ride next day had more of a climb than we anticipated, to 5,000 feet. Alas, *La Navigatrice* didn't do her homework. Yeah, we were pedaling through desert, but the route to Bisbee and back would be mountainous. Six days in a row we would climb above 5,000 feet, and five days in a row we would get rained or snowed on. We left the cacti behind and entered a woodier landscape as we climbed. It was Jim's turn to bonk. From our earliest trips, he insisted I ride in front—he had this notion that if we were to get hit by a car, it would be from behind and hopefully they'd take him out but not me. One of the signs that Jim was failing was the distance between us got greater and greater. Finally, I circled back.

"Why don't we just free-camp here? I'm pooped, too."

"No," he said. "We don't have enough water, we've got to get to the fairgrounds." The look on his face told me this was another of those times where the options were non-negotiable, so we pushed on.

When we got to the town of Sonoita, we headed straight for the campground at the Santa Cruz County fairgrounds. Unfortunately, the women in the front office told us we couldn't camp there that night because we arrived past their 2 p.m. deadline. Huh?

"Bullshit," Jim snorted when I told him. "I bet they just don't want cyclists. Let's go back to town. I'm beat up, we're cold. Let's find a hotel and splurge." I was in no mood to resist so we headed to the big red barn in town.

"You're in luck, we still have a few rooms available," said the friendly host. "And your room includes breakfast and a complimentary happy hour with local wine."

"Hot diggity dog," I said to Jim as he closed the door. "Look at the size of this bathtub; we can both fit. Do we have time for a soak and a nap before happy hour?" I giggled as I plopped down on the soft bed covered in red and white flowers. Jim ran the water in the enormous tub.

"Yes, in that order, and I hope the local wine is good. If we like it, maybe we can buy a bottle to take with us."

"Don't make it too hot, I want to get in with you." I laughed as the steam rose. Jim liked his bath five or ten degrees hotter than I. "I'll sleep while you soak. Wake me when you get out and I'll jump in," I said as I drifted off.

The Sonoita Inn presents as a barn, but inside it's homey and cozy, with lots of horse photos and cowboy decorations. Rested, clean, and warm, we entered the lobby two hours later and found a scrumptious spread of wine, charcuterie, cheese, crackers, grapes, fruit, cherry tomatoes—wow—all laid out on a big wood table.

"Hi, I'm Graham," said a friendly red-headed and freckled man with a thick Scottish accent. A frequent business traveler and a twenty-seven-year resident of Palm Springs, he peppered us with questions. "I can't believe you can really enjoy yourselves on bicycles," he insisted as he drained his wine.

"Here's the thing about long-distance cycling," I countered as I savored some cheese and grapes. "Yes, it's true, the lows can be so low, but when we stop for the day, we get a jolt of exhilaration because we made it, the day's challenges becomes a distant memory, and the challenges of the next day's travails are unknown. Plus we feel really strong and turned on from the workout."

"More power to you," Graham laughed. "I'll leave the highs and lows to you; I'm staying in my Camaro."

Next morning as we filled up at yet another buffet breakfast, we realized what a resource hotels could be over campgrounds—we got two filling meals, plus met interesting people and a staff with tips for where we were headed.

A mile down the road, Jim got a flat on his rear wheel, even with the replaced spoke.

"The Continental rim has a tear. I've got to find a better tire," Jim sighed. "Why couldn't this have happened in Tucson? Did you bring your sewing kit?" He asked.

"Of course, whaddya got in mind?" I asked.

"Either I sew the tear, or we bike back to Tucson for a new tire," he explained. So we propped the bikes on the side of the road and Jim sewed the tear. Boy, was I impressed.

We entered grazing ranch land with an eventual end to the desert cacti—a sign we should have paid attention to. It was too cold for the cacti to survive the winters. We saw a sign for one vineyard and the construction of another one amid scrub oak and manzanita. There were even scrappy pine trees around.

We scored a campsite on the banks of Parker Lake with a view of the water. Some boaters, some campers, but most were day-use picnickers packing up to go home just as we pitched the tent. The ranger came down to get our money before we even finished setting up.

"There's a big storm forecasted for Monday, but these clouds tell me it's coming tomorrow," he said as he filled out our camping pass. "I'd advise against taking those scrawny little wheels up over the pass, it's not paved and turns to mud pretty fast. Plus, Garden Canyon is narrow and likely to wash out," he added as he walked away.

Disappointed by the news, next day we retraced eleven miles of yesterday's ride and got soaked traveling east through Fort Huachuca Military Base, but at least we were on paved roads and didn't experience any flash floods or washouts. And again the next day, we put in several hours slogging our way through pelting rain, finally toward the end of the ride I bonked.

"I can't do this anymore—two days of rain and cold, and all this climbing, I want to go home," I yelled, discouraged, to Jim as he came up next to me.

"Don't give up," Jim urged. "Remember how much fun Kathy said Bisbee is gonna be? We're almost there, less than ten miles."

"Yeah," I sighed, "but how much of a climb do we have over those ten miles? I've no idea. I'm not sure which is worse—all the unexpected climbing, or the goddamn cold and rain. Can't we just free-camp and get to Bisbee tomorrow?" I whined.

"There's not enough vegetation for us to hide out here, it's too barren, we've got to go on," Jim pointed out. He was right, there wasn't much to hide behind. So I steeled myself, huffing and puffing up another 1,000 feet.

I was so relieved to finally see Welcome to Bisbee. Only problem was it was another five miles to our destination.

Chapter 19

Bisbee, like Tucson, is quite spread out. Thanks to our friend, Kathy, we planned to spend that night in a camper van. After a final climb up an alluvial fan, still in the rain, we pulled into The Shady Dell Vintage Trailer Court.

It was like we'd entered a time warp—a small asphalt lot surrounded by trailers from the 30s, 40s and 50s, each with tiny white picket fences protecting the trailer hitches and decorating the grassy patches. Vintage lounge chairs and two bright yellow vehicles—a 1940s Plymouth sedan and a 1950s Ford pickup—not sure if they were drivable or just added decoration. We met the new owners, a young couple with a baby who recently bought the place from the guy who created it. They had remodeled each of the campers and set them up. Rather than being assigned, customers get to pick which camper they stay in.

Our first choice was a seventeen-foot 1957 El Ray, but as we started unpacking, it felt too crowded so I high-tailed it to the front office and got the green light to switch to the thirty-three-foot, 1951 Spartan Mansion. Instead of reloading the bikes, we just portaged our gear, back and forth, in the rain. Not only was it bigger, but the Mansion was happier—restored to its original glory with a red and white color scheme complemented by the sparkling golden wood paneling. The fridge was bright red, the chenille bedspread had a huge red heart, a fifties-era television rigged to play VHS tapes of fifties-era movies and TV shows.

Oh, it was so nice to be outa the rain. We had a lot of damp gear and draped it everywhere before we took off to explore Bisbee. Fortunately, the rain stopped, but central Bisbee was two miles uphill, past a horrible scar. Ironically called the Lavender Mine, it's 850 feet deep, a mile long, and almost a mile wide. I walked by stunned—how and why do we humans think it is okay to deface our planet so? The pit mine diminished my enjoyment of Bisbee. And my thighs ached as we climbed. We poked around and Jim picked a beat-up old saloon full of locals. We tried a local beer, Electric Ale, but we had to beat a hasty retreat—too much cigarette smoke. Jim found a mineral store run by a wizened old desert rat. Light poured in from the bank of windows along the storefront, highlighting the rows of dusty glass-topped cases of the more valuable gems, while shelves of open cardboard boxes of the less expensive items lined the walls. It reminded us of the California Mineral Museum when it was housed in the top floor of the San Francisco Ferry Building.

Brewery Gulch was a quirky neighborhood—an assortment of houses in all kinds of fixer-upper states. Lots of artistic touches; beautiful nineteenth-century decorative woodwork and gargoyles. We had to be careful navigating the unpaved streets muddy from the rain. We bought homemade Italian sausage plus local beer in an old-fashioned corner grocery store with a butcher. Then we had to descend back down the hill. Jim was quite happy, he loved the vintage camper, found the town interesting, and rescued me from a meltdown. We listened to vintage music on a fake old-fashioned radio that plays CDs.

After spending several hours hemming and hawing the next morning about whether to go and brave the wind or stay at Shady Dell and wait it out, we decided to go. We got everything packed, then Jim couldn't find his helmet. We looked in every cabinet and drawer, under the trailer, in the bushes. No helmet. Then Jim figured it was likely in our first pick the day before. Jim had unpacked about half his gear before we decided to switch, so he guessed it was in there. Trouble was, the owners were gone and the sign at the office said they wouldn't be back in the late afternoon. It felt like a repeat of Ireland when we left our fuel bottles behind in the airport. So we spent another day exploring Bisbee, and sure enough, Jim's helmet was in a closet in the El Ray.

Bisbee was a trip, so many different parts to the town. The first one we saw was the business district along Highway 92, just a typical collection of storefronts strung out along the road. Then we entered the old business district of beat-up buildings dating from the twenties. Some were empty, but many were artist living/working spaces. That's where Shady Dell was located. A large part of Bisbee is the enormous pit, the remains of the raping of the land for copper and whatever. It was very hard for me to warm up to Bisbee with that awful scar upon the land. Next is tourist Bisbee, the center of the old town with shops, restaurants, museums. Quaint, with lots of art and vintage shops. Leading up a side canyon to the east is what I'll call Brewery Gulch Bisbee, a neighborhood built on the remains of nineteenth-century miner housing. A few were in good shape, but most were in such disrepair it was surprising to note signs of habitation.

On our way out of town the next day, we got to see yet another Bisbee, one of a comfortable collection of modest houses in a flat, sprawling neighborhood. Signs of people of independent and artistic character, but with a homey feel. We couldn't take the time to explore; the icy rain motivated us to keep moving. It only got worse as we descended 2,000 feet, the wind sliced right through our layers. My fingers went numb riding the brakes, though not as bad as the time we climbed Mt. Etna. We blasted through Tombstone, nothing enticed us to stop, in better weather we would have had a jolly time.

"Let's keep going," Jim yelled through the wind. "Maybe we can make it to Sonoita."

"That's another forty miles," I yelled back, "and we've already done more than twenty. We might have to free-camp."

"I'd rather push on through to a nice warm bed," Jim insisted. Again I had to admit he was right.

Six hours of cycling later, we pedaled up to the hotel sore and fatigued but happy to have made it. Regrettably, the nice lady at the inn told us there were no rooms.

"And you're not gonna find any rooms available between here and Tucson. Sorry kids, but there's a movie being filmed here." It was well after 2 p.m., so we even didn't try the fairgrounds but headed south on Papago Springs Road.

No happy hour tonight, we stopped at the mini mart, the only store in town. As we loaded the food in our panniers, a young man in dusty clothes walked up with a horse and a mule.

"Hey," he said, "it's so nice to meet like-minded travelers."

"Like-minded?" Jim replied, laughing. "I'd say there's a big difference between bikes and beasts, riding versus walking."

"Well, I mean, no car," he explained. "It's nice to see somebody experiencing this country without a motor. I've been on the road for ten months. I left North Carolina last April, making my way to San Diego. I'm going to stay with a friend for six months and try to write a book about the trip. I take notes along the way. Where are you headed now?" he asked.

"We're heading south, to get to forest service land to free-camp," I answered. "We tried the fairgrounds but they wouldn't let us camp because we arrived too late in the afternoon."

"That's odd," he replied. "I arrived past four and they're letting me stay."

"See, I told you," Jim turned to me. "I bet it was our bikes."

I turned to the guy, "Why do you have both a horse and a mule?" I asked, a little sheepishly, for the question made me feel like a Mosquito.

"Well I carry a lot of gear, and a teepee, as you can see. Two beasts allow me to alternate the weight and pace them."

"How far do you average?" Jim asked. "Do you ever run out of water?"

"About fifteen miles a day," he volunteered. "And I've never run out of water. I just walk up to any farm or house I pass and ask. Nobody's ever said no yet."

"Wow, I guess that's because you're so unique, with the animals."

Anxious to set up camp before dark, we bid adieu, amazed at the guy's stamina.

* * *

Next morning we awoke among the creosote and manzanita bushes to temperatures in the twenties, our water frozen solid, our bikes covered in frost, even the fly of our tent was frozen and crusted. We had to break camp with no breakfast because we couldn't melt the ice. We were getting real tired of cold and wet. Arizona kept the surprises and discomforts coming. We retraced the path to the site of our first night of free-camping, north of Vail. It was a nice spot,

2,000 feet lower, we were looking forward to warming up, though the forecast was for yet more rain.

We battened the hatches before we hit the sack, but when we climbed out of the tent in the morning, everything was again covered in frost. We were incredulous, the weather we hit on this trip. Jim got punchy, cracking wise about the cold and the tent.

"I'm gonna write to Sierra Designs," he snickered, "and tell them their tent is 100 percent effective in keeping out rain, in the Sahara." I laughed and he kept going. "You call this thing a tent? Ha, it's just a piece of exercise equipment: work out to set it up, work out to take it down." he yelled as he took it down, keeping me in stitches while I made pancakes for breakfast with margarine, sugar and, oh yes, dirt. That went over big, fortunately the laughter continued,

"You call yourself a cook? You're a poisoner. If I don't die of cold, I'm gonna die of food poisoning," I laughed a little less but sucked it up.

Sitting nervously on the plane as it climbed up and over the Tucson Mountains the next day, I wondered if the bumpy arrival had been a warning: Go Back! I turned to Jim.

"I assumed the Arizona desert would deliver pretty similarly to our winter experiences in Southern California, but I didn't pay attention to elevation. Only the first and last nights were we below 3,000 feet. That's what the Garmin says anyway."

"Are you sure you're reading the Garmin data correctly?" Jim asked as he tilted his chair back. Jim bought me the Garmin for Xmas 2003, a cute little handheld device with a one-inch by one-inch screen. State of the art at the time, I could change out tiny memory cards that covered vast

Chapter 19

areas—several states or an entire country, for example. Jim attached it to my handlebar so I could read it while cycling. I zoomed in for detail and zoomed out for the big picture, but the screen was so small, it was still nice to have paper maps. I soon became a Total Data Junkie. In my journals, I added new items to my trifecta of miles, time, and max elevation: max speed, average speed, moving time, stopped time, elevation climb, elevation descent. And I loved it all. Curiously, elevation descent turned out to be most surprising. Paper maps rarely included elevation change data.

"Yeah," I insisted. "The moral of this trip is another lesson for my list, let's see, that's number twenty-four. Never Assume. I used my maps to design the loop, assuming the Arizona desert was the same elevation as Southern California. But the Garmin is educating me otherwise. Sheesh. Do you realize for six nights in a row we were above 5,000 feet? In Death Valley we only camped that high once."

"Well, that park ranger at the lake said the rainfall was exceptional," Jim answered. "We didn't plan for that, we never had rain in Death Valley, that's for sure. But we made it, we're heading home, the weather didn't beat us, and the warm hotel rooms sure helped."

"Yeah, you're right about that," I replied. "Think how much harder it would have been if we camped every night."

"We just gotta be a bit more vigilant about weather and elevation," Jim sighed. "So where we going next, and when?" he laughed as he sipped the complimentary wine.

South of Tucson

The Shady Dell, Bisbee

Free camping south of Sonoita

TWENTY

Anne & Jim's Second Great Adventure

Bright and early on Valentine's Day 1977, I slid out of bed as quietly as I could to avoid waking Jim. He had been trying to finish his BA at UC Berkeley since the previous summer and driving the night shift for Eagle Cab, while I worked 11 a.m. to 7 p.m. at Blue Print Service on Second Street in downtown San Francisco. That meant we were pretty much ships passing in the night Monday through Friday. On impulse the day before, I bought one of those thirty packs of school Valentine cards I remembered from childhood. Before I left for work, I hid them, individually, where he would find them as he got ready for work—in his shirt pocket, shoes, on his razor, in the coffee pot, the sports section of *The Chronicle*, etc. As I slipped each in, I got a big kick out of imagining his surprise; I was tingling like a second-grade girl tucking them into construction-paper envelopes.

Later, he told me one fell out of his jacket pocket as he went to make change for his first fare of the evening. We had been talking about getting married off and on for a few months, and my silly Valentines provided the spark. The next six months became a whirlwind of wedding preparation. The last Saturday in August, under redwood trees in the Northern California town of Cazadero, we tied the knot, then took off for Europe.

We wanted to travel as far and as long as our money would take us, but frankly, we didn't have much cash; a month was it. So we put ourselves on an austerity plan, and Jim postponed finishing at Cal to work extra shifts. By August, we saved enough for four months' travel if we could stick to a budget of twenty-five dollars a day. Jim bought the Harvard students' go-to guide for budget travel at that time, *Let's Go*, we bought tickets to fly via the cheapest option at the time, Icelandic Airlines, and we bought two four-month unlimited-travel train tickets.

From August to December, we traveled from Scotland in the north to Morocco in the south, from Lisbon in the west to Vienna in the east. It was easy back then—even the sleeper trains weren't difficult to book at the last minute. We'd hop off the train and look for the closest lodgings, not wanting to walk too far lugging our two suitcases (wheeled suitcases hadn't been invented yet). We mostly booked rooms in what the Europeans called pensions—small, family-run establishments, what one would call shabby chic today. I don't remember ever having a private bathroom. Our lodgings averaged $10 a night. We quickly settled into a pattern wherever we went: hop on a train in the morning, stop before dark, find a room, and stroll the neighborhood for a decent restaurant for dinner. Stay one to three days, depending on how interesting and fun the place was, then on to the next one. If we knew we wanted to cover real distances, like from Algeciras to Barcelona, or Lucerne to Vienna, we booked a sleeper car.

Each country had its own advantages and challenges for the budget traveler. After taking a ferry from England, we settled into an economical, lovely houseboat on the Turfhaven Canal in Hoorn, run by a friendly widow. When we discovered how tiny the country was, we opted to stay in the houseboat and use our train pass to visit Amsterdam and the Kröller Müller Museum. But Dutch prices broke our budget, we couldn't last four months if we continued in the Netherlands or further north. The next day, we took a train south and spent the rest of our trip in countries with lower prices and better exchange rates.

Chapter 20

Some places were easy. The absence of a language barrier in the UK helped, though sometimes Jim and I weren't sure we were listening to our native tongue. The cheapest B&Bs were quite rundown with lousy mattresses, though the Brits always offered a full breakfast—eggs, bacon, fried tomatoes, toast, butter, jam, and the god-awfullest instant coffee I can still smell—served by surly waitresses, often in the dingy basements of beat-up old establishments. In London, the monuments and historic buildings matched the cheesiness of our budget lodgings; centuries of black soot covered everything. We found pubs the best place to get our main meal of the day, with reasonably priced standard fare like meat pies, fish and chips, stews and roasts, washing it down with warm pints of beer.

Some places were disappointing—Spain, for example. Franco had recently died, but his ghost lived on. There was a dreary pall, most everyone wore funereal black clothes and paranoid faces; the country conveyed a sadness that made it impossible for us to enjoy ourselves. So we split for Portugal, and loved it. The poverty in Lisbon was palpable, but the streets were joyful—the colors brighter, the aromas delectable, and the laughter infectious, proving money doesn't necessarily buy happiness.

We were in southern Portugal when Jim proposed Morocco on a lark. We took the ferry, and the six-hour bus ride felt like a time machine, traveling back a century with each hour, to enter a world unlike any other we had ever been in. Jim was keen on spontaneity and discovery, but we found ourselves out of our element; the streets felt dangerous and we were intimidated almost everywhere we went. In Rabat, a stranger accosted Jim in the old city center and we were surrounded within seconds. We didn't speak Arabic, no one volunteered English, but one man offered to translate French. The accoster said it was against his religion to have his picture taken and insisted we hand over our Pentax K1000 camera for him to destroy. Through the translator, Jim was able to negotiate and give the accoster the roll of film. Too bad, since we had pictures on the roll going back to Lisbon. At least we hung on to the camera. Feeling we were in over our heads, we returned to Europe the next day.

Other places were a mixed bag. Italy was a country of art, riches and antiquities, but we learned the hard way that we couldn't eat dinner in restaurants. At that time, the expectation was that diners ordered both a pasta dish and a meat entrée, making dinner the equivalent of our daily budget. So we ate pastries with espresso for breakfast and pizza slices from sidewalk vendors for dinner, saving our precious pennies for museums, art, and music.

But the countries we visited were never, ever as much fun as France.

We had a blast everywhere we went in the Hexagon. Thanks to the horrid prices in the Netherlands, we escaped to a *Let's Go* best budget recommendation, Henri IV on Ile de la Cité. They put us on fifth floor, the top, in a room with a slanted ceiling that Jim repeatedly bumped his head against. There was a flimsy, two-inch mattress on a squeaky metal bed. The toilet was on the opposite side of an interior metal stairwell, requiring we leap over a two-foot gap with a view of the ground floor five floors down. But we were steps from *Le Pont Neuf*, the center of the prettiest city in the world. We were traveling on the cheapest budget possible at the time, but we were in heaven.

It was in France that I learned how to enjoy good cooking. Jim had started teaching me while we were dating,

Chapter 20

taking me to his favorite French restaurants in the city, and some in the East Bay, like *La Bouillabaisse* in Alameda and *Chez Panisse* in Berkeley. We arrived in France at *Gare du Nord* station, disembarking onto wet city streets sparkling in bright sunshine from overnight rains. Later that evening, we peered in the windows of *Le Volcan*, on the corner of *Rue Mouffetard* and *Rue Thouin* in the Latin Quarter. It was hoppin', so we looked at each other. "Dinner here?" Jim asked.

"Looks promising, it's popular," I replied. In we went to discover the fixed price menu, a three-course dinner, with a half carafe of wine, basket of French bread, and tip included, for nineteen French francs, four dollars each. A slow, lazy, delicious meal unfolded in a room filled with boisterous students on a Saturday night. Each course was a petite piece of art; quite small portions, but lovingly created and delicious. We were hooked. After ten days in Paris, we decided we should take a train and check out the rest of the country.

On our first stop in the provinces, Saumur, we learned that local churches were a thrifty alternative to expensive châteaus. The tenth-century château could only be viewed on a scheduled tour with a group, but the doors of the churches with stunning artwork inside, were open. We toured them at our pace, checking out the art, the altars, stations of the cross, chapels, tiles, etc., and left when we were ready.

France was easy, France was fun, France fit our budget. France was surprising, delicious, intoxicating; a country of people who make choices based on pleasure and an appreciation for the finer things in life. And the French embrace it, from the poorest to the richest—the sensibility of the importance of pleasure and beauty being a part of daily life is pervasive. We traveled on a shoestring budget and felt rich beyond our dreams. When I die, I don't want to go to heaven. I want to go to France.

We stayed in some places even shabbier than *Henri IV* in Paris. For example, the lodgings inside the walled city of *Carcassonne* were so expensive we settled for the nearby and flea-bitten ragtag town of *Castres*. The pension didn't even have toilets in the bathroom, just a hole in the floor. But we didn't mind, it was close enough and cheap enough to visit the walled city by day and sleep within our budget at night.

Back in our room overlooking the *Loire* on our last night in Saumur, Jim announced, "I want to see how far off the track we can really get tomorrow. I want to try to break free of the rigidity of the train schedules. Let's take the train to the end of the line, then take a bus and hitchhike until we get to a place as far off the track as possible." By now, I knew Jim well enough not to be surprised at his desire for spontaneity, and who was I to object to hitchhiking? I had thumbed across the country with a friend for my brother's wedding in '73.

"I'm game if you are," I replied, thinking that there was only so much real estate between here and the Atlantic.

The train took us to Quimper, a lovely Breton fishing town. Then Jim picked a bus to the northeast. Thirty minutes later, when the bus took a left at the fork in the road, he hopped up and rang the bell to stop. "I want to go to the right," he explained as we unloaded our two suitcases. I turned his suitcase sideways and sat down on it. "Now what?" I asked, confused.

"Hitch," Jim said, "I want to go where buses can't get to." Within minutes, a lady, probably in her fifties, screeched to a halt and jumped out of her car, a dusty green *Citroën 2CV*. "*Allez, allez!*" she called out to us with a big smile on her face. We had no idea what she had in mind and we didn't ask. Jim tried to tell her his plans but he couldn't get a word in edgewise—she barely stopped talking. Jim seemed to get a handle on what she had in mind, but I didn't.

Twenty minutes later, she pulled in front of the *Hotel du Styvel,* a charming three-story hotel/restaurant overlooking the *Port de Plaisance* in the seaside town of *Camaret-sur-Mer.* Turns out, our driver was friends with the owners of the establishment and knew they were keen to get any guests they could this time of year. The next three days were the best of our honeymoon. We had a third-floor room with a view of fishing boats bobbing in the quay and the Celtic Sea beyond. We walked to a chapel that rose at the far end of the jetty and found it was built in the twelfth century.

Out for a walk the next morning, we spied a squat door in an old stone building down an alley. Over the locked door was a modern sign for Kronenbourg beer, and to the left was a curved-wood signed painted with white letters: Café—Jeux—Bar—0 20 100 0. Intrigued, we went around the back of the building and entered a field of precisely arranged boulders, most taller than us. The French call them *menhirs,* a Celtic term meaning "long stone." There are scores across Brittany and were dozens in this field. As we followed the long line of boulders, the rough outline of a castle led us to the bluffs. Dating from the eighteenth century, it was destroyed during World War II. Inside, we heard the ocean surf of Plage de Pen Hat, a pristine sandy beach that we had to ourselves for the next two days; sunbathing, castle-building and picnicking.

There were many more wonderful surprises in France. We toured prehistoric cave art in Les Eyzies, attended a choral midnight mass on a rainy Saturday night in the

Pyrenees, watched an Armistice Day parade in Arles, and returned to Paris for our final five days in Europe. France changed us in a way no other country did. We had fun in a lot of countries, but we fell in love with France. We flew back to California in January as different people than when we left. France and its sensibilities were imprinted in our hearts, on our souls. How we shopped, cooked and ate, the wine we drank—we did it all differently, *a la Francaise*. It took us twenty years to return, and our second trip would prove to be an even bigger game changer than our first.

Picnicking on the banks of the Loire

Biking to Fontrevaud L'Abbaye

Hiking in Wales

Biking in Arles

Stopping for two pints near Cambridge

TWENTY-ONE

Beyond the US #2: Pub Crawl

It'd been eight years since our bike tour of the Dordogne. That idyllic experience inspired us to try to repeat the fun. Physicality is what we got instead, lots of it, testing us in ways we never imagined and revealing to us a different view of the world. Like childbirth, the challenges dimmed with time, gave us strength, and made us more confident. But surprises kept coming, every trip.

Ireland would be no different. We left with the usual, first-time visitor assumptions: emerald green, music, ancestors, and beer. The reality would be more nuanced, often exasperating, and much richer.

After clearing customs at 8:30 a.m., we pushed our loaded carts to an empty corner of the Dublin airport parking garage and started assembling the bikes. Half an hour later, as the cars started filling up the spaces all around us, a security guard pulled up in a little electric cart.

"Hey, what are you doing in here? You've got to move. If you stay here you have to pay for this spot."

"We're setting up our bikes. Got any idea where to?" Jim asked in frustration.

"Yeah, see that corner, way over there? There's a big space behind some posts. You can probably fit in there," he offered as he drove away, shaking his copper-topped head from side to side.

It took us twenty minutes to portage the splayed-out gear, another two hours to finish set up. We planned to bike fifteen miles through Dublin to its southern edge—not the brightest plan, especially considering we were operating on fumes after flying from SFO overnight. I had an ominous feeling we weren't as prepared for this trip as we should be.

Our early years of excessive preparation gave way to a lackadaisical approach.

Immediately, I found navigation impossible, and I had only myself to blame. I bought maps, but the scale wasn't detailed enough. Fifteen miles took three hours, I repeatedly took wrong turns, down squirrelly streets that curved every which way. I stopped at an intersection with no signs and five streets coming in at all angles.

"What's up?" Jim barked at me from behind.

"I'm not sure which street to take," Jim's impatience only made it worse, so I picked a road, got a mile and found us back at the same intersection. Oh, I had to get better maps, but where, and when?

It was past five when we finally pulled into the Clondalkin's Camac Valley Caravan & Camping Park, a lotta words but not much else. No store, no restaurant. We had hoped to buy fuel in the campground store. So after pitching our tent, we forced our weary bodies to walk to town, to dine at the Steering Wheel. It was a Saturday night, and the place was hoppin'.

Irish pubs are as much community centers as watering holes. The food was filling and reasonably priced, if a bit heavy on the starches (meat pies, fish and chips, stews, etc.). The place was filled with families dressed in their Sunday finest. Looked like many were celebrating First Communion; little girls in lacy white dresses with matching white shoes while the boys had on crisp, white shirts and navy pants with matching bow ties. I could have watched for hours, but we had to sleep.

We settled for a cold breakfast in the morning. Hot coffee or tea shaves the rough edges off camping for me. Plus, the campground didn't have picnic tables and the grass was drenched in dew. There is nothing homey about an Irish campground.

Chapter 21

An hour later, I had a blowout on my rear tire, right at a farm where an older couple were crossing their cows, and we were in their way. I had to push my laden bike to avoid being trampled on. Suspicious with stern faces, they kept an eye on us as they moved the cows. Jim patched the tire while I watched three baby cows nursing. Each calf had a different personality: one was a rookie with milk all over its face, one was a slow, steady plodder, the last was an aggressive tit-grabber, going from teat to teat and back again.

In the gorgeous Wicklow Mountains, a road sign warned of work delays up ahead. We found four men, one sweeping while the other three watched. A sign at the summit said, Vartry House—Highest Pub in Ireland. We looked at each other and said, "Why not?" Leaning our bikes against an empty picnic table, we went in for Guinness and tea. Like the night before, the pub was warm and cozy–we could have stayed there for hours.

We stopped at a campground on the Avenmore River and pitched our tent not too far from a bright red and green caravan wagon with yellow trim, a kind of Irish Conestoga wagon drawn by one huge horse. Curious, I followed the woman from the wagon into the ladies' room. A petite brunette in a thick green jacket and black rubber boots answered my questions politely.

"We average about seven miles a day, for five days; the steep roads limit where we can ride. The rental firm provides maps. It's a lot of work, but our girls love taking care of the horses. They have to be cleaned, combed, fed morning and night. Five days is long enough."

Dinner in the pub the night before was so nice we decided to dine out again our second night. Hell, we still hadn't bought camping fuel, so we walked to Jacob's Well, an animated pub with the television on.

"Jim," I asked, "what's on the television?"

"I'm not sure," he replied as he sipped his Guinness. "It looks like rugby." An amiable and handsome man seated to our left corrected him.

"Irish football," he said. "It's a cross between rugby and soccer with a round ball that must be touched by the toe before being held in the hands. Three points for going into the net and one point for going through the uprights."

"Never heard of it before. Are there many teams?" Jim asked.

"Oh yeah, every county in Ireland has a team, and this one . . ." I stopped listening and pulled out my journal, filling several pages as the Irish man educated Jim on the game.

Again, we had a cold breakfast next morning, ugh. Pubs were great, but we really needed to buy some fuel. And we really needed better maps. At a 1,625-foot pass, there was an unmarked, unnamed four-way intersection—I really had no idea which one to take.

In Aughrim, we found a newsstand that had better maps, a hardware store that sold liters of camping fuel, and O'Toole's Traditional Bar, with a yellow brick fireplace and view of the river. Between the screwy roads and the pubs, we weren't putting in the miles we expected. We continued through rich green farmland. In Gorey, we bought a bottle of French wine and ingredients for Irish lamb stew, then nipped into O'Brien's Pub before we headed to a campground on the Irish Sea. The thatched-roof pub had an ancient bar with a shiny worn dance floor, a lit fireplace, and a Pennsylvania license plate over it.

Chapter 21

"My cousin sent it over," replied the gray-haired bartender to my query.

"What do you have on tap besides Guinness?" I asked.

"Bulmer's cider is popular with the ladies. If you've never had it, I suggest you start with a half pint. It has a bit of a kick to it." It went down like Little Jesus in Satin Pants. Not a fan of warm beer, it was easy to order tea, but Bulmer's became my livelier alternative.

On our way to the coast, we passed a solitary male dressed all in black. Small and thin, from behind I guessed he was twenty. As we passed, I saw a worn-out shell of a man, flushed, sweaty, and greasy. Already drunk, he turned away. We would encounter many solitary drunks on the roads and in the pubs in the weeks ahead.

Then I got another flat. As Jim repaired it, Mr. Bailey, a most loquacious farmer in whose driveway we stopped, approached us.

"Can I help ye?"

"No, thanks," Jim replied. "The front wheel is easy to repair."

"This is my driveway you're sittin' in. I'm Mr. Bailey. Run a small farm," he volunteered. "I've only fifty sheep just now," he went on, "but about to supplement them with windmills. Sheep don't pay the rent these days, no, they don't. This farm's been in the family, practically since Cromwell, and my kids have no interest in farming, but I'll not let us lose it on my watch."

On he went for the ten minutes it took Jim to change the flat. Had he invited us in for a drink, or a meal, or the night, I'm sure we would have said yes in a heartbeat—he was so sweet. But he didn't.

Finally, on our third night, we could cook in camp.

Problem was, neither of us had the fuel bottles that screw on to the WhisperLite burner. Where could they be? We checked every pannier, twice, three times. I remembered the airport parking garage - was it possible we left them there, when the security guard forced us to move? Now we had food but no way to cook it.

"Let's just eat whatever we have that doesn't require cooking," I sheepishly suggested.

"No, I'm hungry, I want a real meal." I rolled my eyes — nice food is much more important to him than me. The tone of his voice told me to listen. "I'll ride back to town," he fumed. After he left, I decided to start the bottle of French wine early only to discover it was sweet, couldn't drink it.

Truly remarkable, I thought, *we must have left the fuel bottles in the airport garage. Crazy roads, lousy maps, worn-out tires that should have been replaced.* The results of lousy preparation were piling up. Lesson #25: Preparation, Preparation, Preparation. To top it off, soaking wet campgrounds with no tables and cold showers were compounding our mistakes. Jim returned in thirty-five minutes with Chinese takeaway. The food was lousy. Needless to say, it was not one of our better evenings.

Next morning, after another cold breakfast, I looked at Jim. "Maybe we should just do without cooking? The pubs are terrific."

"We don't go very far without seeing one," Jim admitted. "But I'd still like to buy a stove if we can find one."

Twin church steeples guided our route into Wexford, a bustling medieval port town. Jim bought two new tires and a cheap stove. After lunch, we found ourselves flummoxed at yet another unmarked five-road intersection.

Chapter 21

"Look at that yellow building," Jim pointed. "Looks like a pub. Let's get directions in there."

"What'll you have?" asked the barrel-chested bartender inside the Coach Inn. When we told him a half pint of Bulmer's and a Guinness he smiled.

"Good choices, sounds like you've been here before," he said and laughed. He was so nice we sat at the bar.

"We've been here four days. When I requested something on tap yesterday, they suggested Bulmer's."

"The sign of a woman with taste," he continued. "I can pick you out. I'm the fifth generation to run this establishment, been in my family over 120 years."

It was a good thing we had the lovely meal and a late afternoon pub stop, for the evening didn't go so well. I'm not sure which was worse: the pathetic, bare-bones, no tables, sopping wet field that called itself a campground and restrooms too dreary to shower in, or that, again, we had no warm dinner. Try as he might, Jim could not get the cheapo stove to generate a flame hot enough to cook.

Next morning as we broke camp in the rain, everything was damp. After lunch, we hit a brutal stretch. It seemed the Irish have yet to learn of switchbacks. Maybe they built roads straight up because it required less asphalt? Over and over again I had to walk. In the rain. I hated stopping; once I did I couldn't get back in the saddle until the slope flattened. The worst was if I encountered someone as I was pushing—so embarrassing.

In Bunmahon, we stopped when we saw five cyclists huddled on the side of the road, adding layers. They advised us against staying on the coast to Cork because it a bank holiday weekend was coming up. Not only would all accommodations be booked, but traffic would be thick, drunk, and dangerous.

We departed with thanks for the tip and when we passed the charming Seaview Guesthouse, still in the rain, I looked at Jim, he looked at me. "Why not?" Maureen welcomed us in and told us to come down for afternoon tea after we settled in. The house was on a bluff with a view of the ocean out one window; the other, a road with an old stone bridge, Roman aqueduct style, leading to the mountains. A foyer divided the family's private rooms from the hallway with five guest rooms.

We showered, dressed, and grabbed our rain jackets, figuring we'd walk to town for dinner after tea. Well, the tea turned out to be a full meal—a pot of tea accompanied by a huge pile of triangle-cut sandwiches, six mini tarts and two candy bars. What a treat, to be warm and dry and not have to walk in the rain to eat. We did the math—the campgrounds gave us access to a toilet and soggy grass, no picnic table or camp kitchen, and showers, sometimes hot, sometimes not, always extra. As we burrowed under the flowered comforter that night, we decided to change our focus from camping to guest-housing.

Plus, the next morning, Maureen laid out a full Irish Breakfast—eggs, bacon and sausage, toast, muffins, butter, jam, fried tomatoes, juice, and coffee. After profuse thanks we left and biked along the stunning Cork coast only a few miles more before we headed northward inland. As I struggled at yet another crazy intersection, two older men in yellow worker vests stopped to chat.

"Why, you're a lady!" The older man exclaimed, and turning to the younger one, he said, "A lady, riding a heavy bike like that," as he shook his head. They were two characters straight out of *Waking Ned Devine*.

"Where ya from?" he continued, hardly missing a beat. And when Jim said California, well, he had an aunt in Daly City.

Chapter 21

It took us awhile to extricate ourselves. We were learning what to expect every day — great pubs, crazy roads, friendly people, and Irish towns with Old World centers and New World outskirts.

* * *

Stone abounds in Ireland — the walls, barns, houses and churches; vines and flowers grow all over them — out the cracks, along the top, tumbling down the sides. Many build a new, modern house next to the abandoned old one. Every once in a while, we passed an exquisitely maintained stone house and farm with a courtyard. Bushes, trees, flowers, wildflowers everywhere. It would be easy even for me to be a gardener in Ireland.

We biked a road where the hedges were made of fuchsias, six feet tall. When we stopped at a pub in Ardagh, I asked the bartender if she could recommend a nearby guesthouse.

"Well, Kathleen lets rooms in her farmhouse, it's fifteen minutes north of here, by car that is. You might try her place." Warmed from Guinness and tea we headed north in the pouring rain under a canopy of trees on a road with a row of grass down the middle. Kathleen's farmhouse was two-stories, white with gray trim and Doric columns. A tall brunette in a soiled green apron answered the door just past 5 p.m. on that Friday afternoon.

"I'm sorry, I'm filled up with a party of fishermen." Oh, I was so disappointed, and we didn't have a Plan B.

"Do you know of any campgrounds nearby? We have a tent," I asked out of desperation.

"Well, if you have a tent, you can pitch it in our yard. I'll charge you for tea and breakfast and a shower."

Jim and I looked at each other, thrilled.

"Oh, thank you," I beamed as she led us to a grassy spot surrounded by flowers.

"Will this work? This side is more private. And you're not too far from the front door if you need to use the toilet in the night. After you set up your tent, come in and I'll show you the bathroom and the parlor where I serve evening tea promptly at six. Feel free to sit in the parlor until bedtime." She left us and the rain stopped just as we set up the tent. Less than an hour later, we were in a cozy parlor with a crackling fire, a pot of tea, a pile of ham, tomato and coleslaw sandwiches, and a tray of cookies and mini tarts.

Next morning while enjoying Kathleen's Full Irish breakfast, she approached our table.

"Do you mind if I ask how old you are?"

"Um, I'm fifty-one," I replied, not sure where the conversation was going.

"We don't see many women on bicycles of any age around here," she explained.

In Cooraclare, Tubridy pub lured us in with its golden yellow and bright red trim on the outside. As I scanned the historic posters and vintage dishes inside, an older couple came in. They were from Vancouver, and though he was a former bike racer, she was uneasy, so they rode a tandem and pulled a trailer to carry their gear, chasing the music.

"Be sure to stop in Miltown Malbay, just ahead. It's the best for traditional music," they told us as we left. Miltown Malbay easily had double or triple the number of pubs and hotels than any town yet.

The owner of Kelly's Hotel said, "No bikes in the rooms," and gave Jim directions about where to store them. They were to go in a shed out back. But Jim had other ideas as he

Chapter 21

carried each bike down the hallway, then up two flights of rickety stairs while I lugged the gear.

We came down to a bar filled with locals watching a soccer game, Ireland vs. Israel, for World Cup points, and met Adrian.

"I took a train from Dublin," he volunteered. "Four hours, and stops in Ennis, then takes me two hours to bike here." Adrien had lived in San Francisco for six years and had twin sons in New York City. By this time, we were certain that every living Irish person had relatives in the US. He said Lynch's had the best music.

"Only problem," he warned, "the music doesn't usually start until half ten."

We scored two of the last empty seats at half nine; by ten, it was standing room only. But when the music started, no one stopped talking. The din was deafening. I was so disappointed — we couldn't hear the music well enough to appreciate it. After an hour, we gave up.

The next day, we boarded a ferry at Doolin for Inishmore, the biggest of the Aran Islands. All the signs were in both English and Gaelic; we heard lots of Gaelic spoken. At a gift shop in Kilronan, I asked the elderly clerk if Gaelic was her first language.

"Oh yes, Gaelic is the only language I speak," I suppressed a laugh as we walked away.

The rain started as we set off unloaded, the sky gray and misty, the colors were gray and green with occasional bits of color from wildflowers. Bare, windswept rock everywhere, rock walls enclosing absurdly small plots.

The island became more desolate as we made our way to the western tip. Vast layers of tilted rocks terraced down to crashing waves. Instead of returning to Doolin, we took a ferry north to County Galway and found ourselves biking through bogland strewn with large granite rocks and steep treeless glacier-scraped mountains. The roads were a continual challenge—terrible traffic and inhumane grades, but we adapted and lived large, Irish-style. During the day, we looked for pubs; afternoons, we kept an eye out for guest houses. The Galway landscape changed several times from rocky terrain to rhododendron-saturated tropical jungle to lush grassland.

* * *

It's curious how different one's perspective is from a distance, versus what it really turns out to be when you get there. I certainly knew Ireland was green and rainy but nobody ever told me about the rocks. The abandoned cottages, new homes, walls out and new, and boulders jutting out of the soil. I fell in love with Irish stone.

Jim and I both fell for Irish pubs, even if they were routinely populated with intoxicated Irish bullshitters. The character of the bars varied: polished or beat-up wood, the age of the building, the bar, the chairs, the people, the space of the room or rooms. Intoxicating, literally and figuratively. Our hours in the pubs became the highlight of each day.

Sitting outside a pub in Ballycroy, a man walked by and looked at us.

"Hello! Great day, isn't it?" About 20 percent of the sky was blue, there was a breeze, and it was probably sixty degrees. That makes for great weather in Ireland.

We passed a church with its doors open, went in, and saw the walls were the loveliest shade of a two-toned violet blue. Most of the back wall, behind and above the altar, was a deeper shade. The sidewalls were mostly a medium yellow-beige. It all made for a celestial affect; *this church has been delivering reassurance to Irish peasants for centuries*, I mused as I sat there absorbing its beauty.

I hoped to free-camp that night on Belderrig Beach, but there was no sand, only rocks. We turned around for The Yellow Rose Guesthouse. Eileen and her fisherman husband, Ian, supplemented his salary by letting out two spare rooms and their lawn to campers. Both rooms were taken, so we settled for the dinner-but-no-breakfast, pitching-the-tent-in-their-yard option. They had two children, two cats, nine kittens, a dog, and a horse about to foal. We learned all of this from the precocious ten-year-old who kept us company while we set up our tent.

For dinner Eileen sat us at a table with an English couple. Fiona was a schoolteacher, Devin, a university geologist who taught a semester sabbatical at Cal in 1966. Again, the American connection. The meal went by quickly as we compared Irish and California geology, travel, the EU, the new euro. We heard a voice as we sunk into our sleeping bags.

"Hello, still up?" I unzipped my door and saw Eileen's smiling face with both hands extended. "Here you go, dinner includes a night cap of local whiskey."

In the morning, we had cold granola, cold coffee, and took off without seeing anyone. The Irish keep late hours. We rode in bright sunshine on the cliff tops along the North Atlantic coast, arriving in the bustling village of Ballina just before noon on a sunny Friday.

There are always more Irish bodies outside when it's sunny or above sixty degrees. The town center was hosting a three-day French market with stalls of locally-grown products — flowers, root-vegetables, and hardy greens. But no cheese! I don't think the Irish got the bulletin. How can one have a French market without cheese? Just the same, it was lovely, and we gave them credit for trying.

In Gorteen, we shared tea with a couple on holiday from Derbyshire. The hostess left the tea tray closest to me, so when she left I began to pour it.

"Oh no," Henry exclaimed as he came around the table and carried away the tea tray like it was in danger. "Let me help you." He sighed as he poured the tea and milk simultaneously. "See? Like this." I turned to Jim and rolled my eyes. I hate milk in my tea.

Fore was delightful, with a monastery complex from the thirteenth century, lots of history, and a cute little pub run by a woman who'd inherited it from her parents. She had a lilting pattern to her voice, talked and entertained us, saying "Ya, ya, ya" over and over again. She had a Beatles book on the bar because she is sitting next to Ringo in the picture on the cover. She was a twenty-something living in London and was brought in as an extra. I commented on the exquisite wood carving over the back of the bar that looked like it came from a church, and she said she had a man carve it and the seats, and another man upholstered the seats and benches. It was a small pub, much more feminine and intimate than most we stopped in.

The next day, we passed a stone farmhouse complex with a red door. It also had red window trim and red roses. Two dogs came out as I took three pictures, but they didn't bark or bite. Cycling Ireland drove home to me how very much the landscape was shaped by the British invasion and colonization of Ireland. In the east and the Midlands, we passed estates with rock gates were bigger than many homes on the West Coast. Lots of large estates with British names. The farms and plots of the West Coast were small, the landscape littered with tiny, abandoned, one-room rock houses. But there were flowers everywhere. Another of the great pleasures on the trip—the constant presence of flowers, from cultivated gardens to fields of wildflowers.

For our last night, we picked a guesthouse in Swords, on the north side of Dublin, close to the airport with good transit into town. We paused to figure out how to get to our guesthouse and a woman on a bike stopped and offered help. Eileen insisted on leading us to our guesthouse. Only problem was she took us back the way we came. When she realized she had led us astray, she insisted we follow her to a friend's house nearby. She turned into a yard and Mary came out. In they went and called the guesthouse for directions.

When they came out, they invited us in for tea. So we had tea and toast with Mary and Eileen in Mary's very modern kitchen; Corian counters and a table with a Singer sewing machine bottom. Her stove had a big aluminum plate and two massively heavy covers to "protect one" from being burned. We had a lovely tea party, comparing notes and ideas on Ireland and travel. Eileen and Mary were like salt and pepper shakers—about the same age but perky Eileen had jet-black hair with alabaster skin while quiet Mary was a redhead with freckles to match. After tea, Eileen again insisted on leading us to our guesthouse, which turned out to be only one block from where we first met.

We didn't plan it, but found ourselves on our last day in Ireland in Dublin on Bloomsday—16 June—the day made famous by James Joyce in his novel *Ulysses*. My father was a devotee of all things Joycean, told me to be sure to get a drink at Davy Byrnes Bar on Duke Street. We found the place already packed at 11 a.m., with many in Victorian dress and straw hats while gentle, wistful Irish music played in the background. It was a lovely bar, the ceiling had recessed squares of flowers and vines on a burnt yellow background. The two chandeliers in the front of the bar were variations on calla lilies. At the top of the wall behind the bar was a pattern of the letters d and b, a dusty pale shade of blue on a white background.

We sat at a little round table on upholstered bench seats a darker shade of the blue, with black, maroon, and brown. The bartender said hello and wished "Happy Bloomsday" to an elderly man with a trimmed but long beard, who appeared to be a regular. The wall under the bar had what appeared to be the bottom of wine bottles, six columns by five rows, framed with brass trim. Behind us on the wall were several large posters covered in plastic, were Maxfield Parrish-type landscapes. We sat next to three sisters in homemade Victorian dresses from Limerick who celebrated there every year on Bloomsday. The pubbiest of pubs was a most fitting end to our three weeks in Ireland.

Again, another trip turned into an education; not what we expected, but the pleasures outweighed the challenges. The mistake of leaving our fuel bottles in the airport garage was softened by our discovery of eating in pubs. The disappointment of campgrounds erased by staying in homey guest houses. The flowers, architecture, rocks, were all delightful surprises. But the roads, the screwy, insanely steep roads, devoid of signage pretty much ensured I would not choose to pedal this green island again.

The end of a very long first day in Rathdrum

Lunch break

Cows watching Jim patch a flat

Market day in Ballina

TWENTY-TWO

Beyond California #4: Rain and Shine

In 2005, my older sister decided to cash out of California and work remotely from the Big Island of Hawaii. Two years later, we accepted their invitation to visit during my winter break and, no surprise, we brought our bikes. Partly as a result of our experiences in Arizona and Ireland, and partly because Hawaii doesn't have many campgrounds, we left all our camping and cooking gear at home, a first since our maiden trip in the Sacramento Valley in '99. The island is a quirky mixture of tropical paradise and desolate volcanism, towns often separated by significant distances. So we felt we had to book all our rooms in advance—unheard of for us—to lay out the maps and commit to doing a counterclockwise loop of a little more than 300 miles in eight days.

They lived in Waikoloa Village, an easy drive from Kona up the northwestern slope of Mauna Kea. I loved the simplicity, spaciousness, and vibrant colors of their home: lime green living room, yellow kitchen lit up with early morning rays, rose bathroom. My sister inherited our mother's green thumb and so it was fun to see what she was up to in the garden. Piled high on a cookie sheet in the kitchen was her first harvested crop of Kona coffee berries. Turning them into a hot drink was a laborious process, so I offered to help.

First, the bright red berries must be shucked, then roasted (in a pan on the stove top), stirred often, and finally, hand ground. I enjoyed the process and we chatted, having a lot to catch up on, hearing about the details of their island life. Everything seemed pared down, simple, and easy. A couple of hours later came the payoff—brewing and sipping the yummy hot coffee. Kona beans really are unique, both sweet and nutty, and especially tasty so freshly brewed; they reminded me of chestnuts.

While I processed the beans, she put the finishing touches on a traditional holiday turkey dinner with all the trimmings. The red-flowered curtains fluttered in the afternoon breeze as we sat down to dine off our mom's old Franciscan Desert Rose dishes, an incongruous combo—a rich warm dinner meal in a balmy island paradise. After dinner, we chatted, played cards and polished off the champagne.

The next day, we packed up a turkey picnic lunch and drove northeast to Pololu Valley, and a hike down the dramatic cliffs carved out of the oldest volcano on the island. We descended 500 feet in half a mile on switchbacks through tropical forest to a stunning black sand beach. Needless to say, we went a lot slower climbing back up, enjoying the incredible views whenever we took breaks to catch our breath.

Jim wanted to visit the observatory at Mauna Kea. Jim offered to drive up the arid, desolate flanks of the dormant volcano to the visitor center at 9,000 feet. It was cold and we fought the wind to get inside. When we came out an hour or so later, it was snowing. Alas, none of us felt up to continuing the eight miles and additional 5,000 feet to tour the Keck Observatory at the top. The Big Island, about the size of Connecticut, packs incredible diversity of landscape, climate, weather.

On our third morning, we bid adieu and rode our lightly loaded bikes back down to Kailua Kona, the main town on the dry, eastern coast. It reminded me of Death Valley, an arid eight miles of undulating alluvial fans, with cinder cones and fields of crusted red- brown lava dotting the landscape. It wasn't even noon when we arrived at our hotel, but they let us into our room with the air conditioning already on. With a free afternoon, we checked out the pier and hopped on a whale-watcher boat. It was a small, houseboat-sized little number with a deep blue canvas roof and white canvas railings. Jim felt right at home, but the railings were so slight I worried we might get pitched out if the surf was rough or if a whale got too close. The guide requested we stay in our seats, warning us to not abruptly rush from one side of the boat to the other to get pictures. We saw bottlenose and spinner dolphins and two humpback whales—a mother and babe. The view of the coast was entertaining, too; pristine beaches, palm trees swaying in the breeze, low-slung homes with walls of windows to enjoy the view up and down the coast.

I booked our second night at Hibiscus B&B, forty-five miles south of Kona, with 3,500 feet of climbing. We left early, but the sun was out in full force and we were so close to the equator, the rays were brutal. The incongruous sight of Christmas decorations entertained us. One house stuck Styrofoam cups in the chain-link fence to spell out Merry Xmas. Another house had a manger scene built around a little girl's pink plastic vanity, with an image of saintly Mary on the mirror. I had to laugh at that one.

We stopped for a break in the charming town of Kealakekua, got Kona coffee at Java Joe's with a view of the ocean 1,500 feet below, and bought souvenirs at an old-timey five and dime store. A few miles south of town, all signs of humanity disappeared. As we continued, I wondered how bad that night's lodgings might turn out to be.

After thirty-five miles of lonely cycling through a natural reserve, we arrived at a godforsaken landscape of harsh volcanic rocks and sun-bleached shacks. Hawaii Ocean View Estates was the creation of some mad, sadistic, egotistical developers who believed they could coax life out of sharp volcanic rocks, a few plants, and even less water. We could have been on Mars. The coastal road dissected this development, the largest in all of Hawaii, an L-shape about eighteen miles long by eight miles wide. We stopped along the main road in the center of "town"—two restaurants, one mom-and-pop shop, and a gas station—to get directions.

Our B&B, only a half mile further, was run by a most unpleasant, rotund older woman, Cecilia, who supplemented her retirement income renting out rooms.

"Keep your showers to a minimum or pay extra," she warned us, her long, curly gray hair bouncing around her shoulders as she walked us to our room. "All my water has to be trucked in." She reminded me of the unfriendly host we had in Wellington, New Zealand in 2003. I mean, don't 'cha think curmudgeons would steer away from working in the hospitality business?

The B&B offered no kitchen facilities, so we opted to walk back to town for a cooked dinner. Hove reminded me of Bisbee—rough, beat up, and full of eccentrics. The buildings were straight out of the Wild West—sun-bleached wood buildings with covered porches and dusty wood-plank sidewalks. Wizened, eccentric characters shopping, eating, drinking, getting mail, shooting the breeze . . . not necessarily in that order. I enjoyed watching them at the Desert Rose restaurant where we had our standard meal—burgers and fries washed down with beer, while trying not to draw attention to ourselves for being outsiders. *Curious*, I thought, *this hardened, beat-up restaurant has the same name as Mom's pretty pink dishes.*

Breakfast next morning was dull: precooked pancakes with stale macadamia nuts, tepid coffee, and no juice, plus, Cecilia sat down to chat with us while we ate. I mean, how can I enjoy my food if I've got to focus on being phony-friendly to a stranger I already know I don't like? Maybe she forgot the lousy mood she was in when we arrived the day before.

"If you have a few hours, you might head to Pohue Bay Beach, it's about four miles." Before we could reply she got up, "Oh that's right, you don't have a car. Never mind." And drifted off to the kitchen.

The otherworldliness continued as we pedaled through the eastern half of Hove to our next night's stay—another B&B, in Na'alehu. This part of the Big Island is so dry and harsh, so raw and volcanic, it is not for the faint of heart. Trucked-in water, gas, and limp produce, prices through the roof, soil-less volcanic rock; the real estate is cheap and attracts those with little money and lots of gumption. As we pulled up to the B&B, I realized the problem of carrying no camping gear; available lodgings decided our distances.

Between Hove and the town of Volcano, the only place with lodgings was Na'alehu, fifteen miles. From the distance of California, I didn't think we could do two forty-five milers in the heat and with the climbs. Danny welcomed us, and in the next instant, let go with a breathless tirade.

"Don't leave your bikes on the lawn, I've got to mow it. Don't be late for breakfast, not before eight—I'm not ready, and not after nine—I've got lots more to do to run this place." His needs, his rules, his problems. "And no noise in your rooms after 10 p.m." Our room was lovely and spacious, but the building and the grounds were more beat up than shabby chic, looking like Danny needed help on several fronts—maintenance as well as hospitality.

We took off on unloaded bikes for Punalu'u Sweetbread Bakery/Gift Shop/Botanical Garden. Oh, we were hungry and enjoyed the Hawaiian pastries. Then we toured a coffee farm in full swing of roasting the harvested beans before the rainy season. We had been getting by on The Great American Tourist Junk Food diet—greasy, poorly prepared fast/snack food. We were keen for something fresh and healthy. The artisanal baked Hawaiian goods were a delicious surprise. Revved up on free coffee samples, we continued to the coast to picnic at Whittington Beach, an abandoned old pier from the bustling nineteenth-century sugarcane days, now bucolic with statuesque palm trees blowing above an expansive Bermuda-grass lawn. Tide pools attracted sea turtles from the rough surf beyond the rocks.

The ride from Naalehu to Volcano included a 4,600-feet ascent, again in full sun, and the equatorial rays were brutal. Mile after mile, we sweated our way uphill, with one brief respite in Pahala, where cold drinks and ice cream helped, but we still had to get back in the saddle. Volcano marked our introduction to the other side of the island's weather. All Hawaiian Islands have a dry side and a wet side. It was like someone flicked a switch. When we pulled into town, it started raining. We rented a tiny cabin with, for those who are into jungle scenery, wrap-around floor-to-ceiling windows to maximize the view. It gave me the heebie-jeebies looking into the thick darkness, and the air hangs with so much moisture that everything is soggy. Ironic, since we spent hours biking in full sun from Naalehu only to get thoroughly doused in the hour we were outside in Volcano. Everything we unpacked felt damp.

Rain again in the morning; what we rode up yesterday we coasted down today. A twenty-mile, 3,600-foot descent, like the descent down Mount Lassen. A pleasant eighty degrees, our bikes sliced through thick sheets of water. We laughed as we coasted, our clothes plastered to our bodies, our shoes and gloves soggy sponges, looking through steamy glasses out at yet another unique experience.

We got to the fork in the road at Pahoa with time to spare, and since the rain had stopped, we took a detour to the southeast to check out the Star of the Sea Painted Church and see how close we could get to the infamous Kalapana Lava Flow. As we approached the church, we found a dejected young cyclist laying out all his soggy equipment on the sidewalks.

"Hey," Jim said, "how ya doing?"

"Pretty bad," he sighed. "I'm on a trial ride for a planned tour of the mainland with some friends next month and it's just terrible—first day out, and already everything is soaking wet." He raised his gloved hands in exasperation, running his hands through his thick, wet brown hair.

"Doesn't look like any of your gear is waterproof," Jim added. "Pahoa has a hardware store. Buy some garbage bags, then head to the nearest laundromat and dry everything out. Believe me, we know your pain; our first set of panniers weren't waterproof either." Jim tried to laugh and turn it into a pleasantry, but the cyclist wasn't having it. He waved us away as he turned his back to us and back to draping his wet sleeping bag over the chain-link fence. So we, too, turned and soon forgot him, dumbstruck by the beauty of the primitive paintings on the walls and ceiling inside the church. Built in the 1920s, it was moved to its present location in 1990 to avoid being engulfed by a lava flow. By the time we came back out to our bikes, the soggy cyclist was gone. Maybe heading to a store and laundromat. My thoughts turned to our earlier trips where we ended up soaked and miserable. Jim rectified our cheesy first choices quick and bought the best waterproof gear. #26: Quality Equipment Matters.

 Hoping to get to see some molten lava, we continued along the increasingly lonely and rough road along the coast, entering another volcanic no-man's-land until the road was roped off with Danger! Road Closed! We could see the steam wafting above the ocean off in the distance, but we couldn't get close enough to see the lava causing the steam. Plants were long gone, hardened lava was all around us with blue ocean to the left, a rising slope to the east, beautiful blue sky with billowing white clouds above, and lava in folds or cracked broken piles too new for any plants to yet be peeking out.

 So we turned and headed east on Highway 137. I made reservations for two nights at yet another B&B, in Kapoho Bay. The volcanic landscape gave way to a tropical jungle with trees so high and thick we were shaded from the hot sun above as we heard the waves crashing against rocks on our right. Every once in a while, the vista would open up to the ocean and we would see tide poolers, surfers, and picnickers enjoying a day along this stunning coast. There were food trucks at Isaac Hale Park, so we stopped for barbecue pulled pork sandwiches, sharing a rickety folding table with a family from Hilo.

 That night found us sleeping on a four-poster bed so high I needed a footstool to climb in. We had a second-story bedroom with our own porch off the back of a palatial home and a picture-postcard view of Kapoho Bay. We crossed the lawn and settled into a delicious hot tub, watching the snorkelers in the bay. Palm trees and flowers everywhere, birds chirping. Joan, a gorgeous blond, got this showcase house, the most glamorous on the street, as part of her divorce settlement and turned it into a B&B to stay afloat. It was either that or return to nursing, but as she met her former husband as a nurse, I think the bloom was off the rose on that career. Unlike the two sourpusses on the south tip of the island, Joan was a natural hostess, ebullient and happy, we were so glad to have two days there.

Next morning, Jim insisted I stop postponing getting in the ocean and set me up with Joan's snorkeling gear. The beach is natural to Jim, having grown up in San Diego, but I'm a freshwater kind of girl. I hate the way saltwater feels on my skin. But he led me in and it was just amazing. Hawaii means paradise to many, but Champagne Cove is a notch above that; an underwater wonderland before my eyes in this protected cove. I saw a three-foot-long blue fish, as still as a rod, a white-striped eel, and lots of little fish. It makes me sad to write about those blissful two days now, for the unparalleled champagne waters of Kapoho Bay disappeared when Kīlauea erupted in June 2018. All is now under a hardened sea of cooled lava.

We left Kapoho in bright sunshine but got drenched in another warm rain as we made our way through mango orchards on our way to Hilo—the main town on the east coast. It was a lot more fun than Kona, a place of tourists. Hilo was a place of artists, with lots of quirky studios, shops, and stores. We spied a junker car across from our hotel that had weeds growing through it as well as all around it. Jim picked out three yards of a subdued blue and white Japanese cotton print for me to make him a tailored shirt.

Leaving Hilo, we headed northeast, entering a thick, dark, damp rain forest. We passed many abandoned buildings in various states of disrepair being reclaimed by the jungle, with roots and veins climbing and crawling around walls, through windows, over roofs. From time to time, we caught a glimpse of the ocean far to the east and far below. The road was like taffy ribbon, in and out, up and down, following the steep slope carved into gorges by waterfalls. The road had decent shoulders but disappeared on the many old bridges, putting us inches from railings that dropped hundreds of feet. The air was both damp and heavy, and dirty, dirty, dirty. We were continually passed by old gas guzzlers spewing horrid fumes, and by the end of the day, we both had headaches. The gas guzzlers, many behemoth cars from the 1980s, spoke to the economics on the island—junk flows down the economic chain.

Our last night on the road found us in a historic sugar plantation home, the Waipo Wayside B&B. It was white with green trim, had hammocks and rocking loveseats on a big porch, and a gazebo in the middle of a sloping lawn that framed an enticing view of the ocean far below. I was so pleased to discover our bedroom was furnished with bird's-eye maple. It's darker than our set at home, maybe because of the humidity. The sides of the bed curved up and around the mattress. The curtains were old tablecloths. After a day of damp and pollution, it was scrumptious to be holed up in such a lovely setting. The cocktail hour found us in the parlor sharing wine, cheese, crackers, and nuts with the other guests: Holly, a twenty-something social worker from Oregon exploring the possibility of moving to the island, and two other couples, a young couple from Pennsylvania on their honeymoon, and an older retired couple from Germany.

We opted to cycle the Old Mamalahoa Highway from Honokaa to avoid traffic and were rewarded with a view of

Chapter 22

snow-topped Mauna Kea to the south. Later, we spied Maui to the north and went through fields of lava tubes on the descent to Waikoloa.

Thanks to Jim's guidance in Kapoho Bay we opted to spend our last day snorkeling in a protected cove on the coast north of Kona. This time, I was much more at ease, eagerly following Jim into the water; it didn't hurt that there were several families with little kids going out farther and deeper. The shallow waters were packed with lots of small, bright-colored fish darting among the coral and sea urchins, undulating back and forth by the pull of the tide.

We stopped off to buy dinner - champagne and steaks, which Jim cooked. As I drifted off to sleep, I looked back on this trip, yet another unexpected adventure. We managed to keep up with our reservations encircling the island. But if/when we return, I'd skip the camping gear again, but double the days to spend as many exploring as cycling. I was surprised how little of a tan we acquired, we only had two days with a lot of sun; ironically the two longest climbing days, but it wasn't enough to go home with that Hawaiian bronzed look. The TV news that night said the Big Island had double the usual rainfall since we arrived.

Kalani Buddha

Volcano National Park

Kalipana-Kapoho Road

Fruit stand near Pahoa

TWENTY-THREE

Beyond California #5: Roly-Poly Land

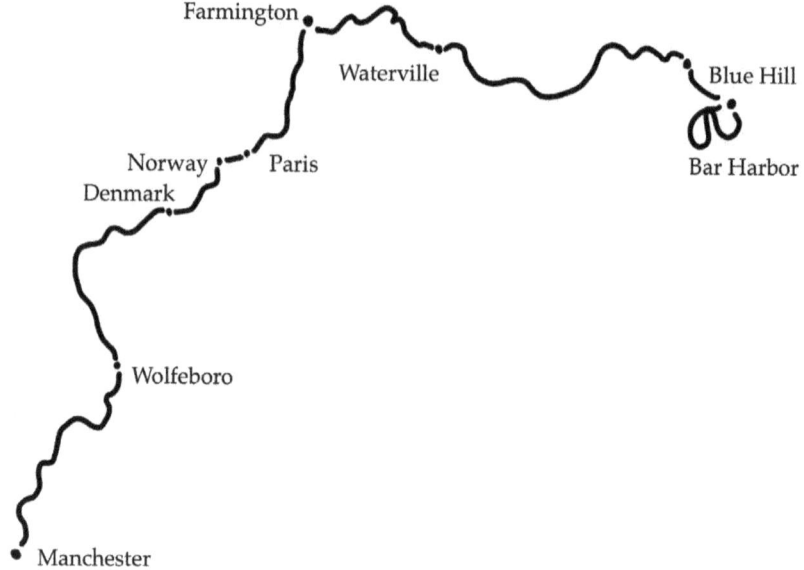

We didn't know it at the time, but our ten-day trek from Manchester, New Hampshire, to Bar Harbor, Maine, would be the last of our Learning-How-To-Cycle-Tour vacations. June 2007 was exactly ten years since our self-guided tour of the Dordogne. Like Hawaii, we again opted to leave the camping and cooking gear at home. The maps and guidebooks indicated we'd have lots of lodging and dining options. Arizona opened our eyes to the benefits of hotels, and Ireland showed us how much more fun it was to let others do the cooking. Unlike Hawaii, though, we made no hotel reservations except for our final destination in Bar Harbor, where we'd be meeting family for a four-day lobster fest.

The TV news at the Manchester airport forecasted rain and thunderstorms for our first few days. Well, we might get drenched during the day, since we knew we could dry out at night. The airport hotel was built to look like an old colonial inn, a common motif in New England. Jim started assembling the bikes as soon as we checked into the room while I sorted, packed, organized the gear, and studied the maps for low-traffic roads Jim so preferred.

Our first day of riding was humid, like riding through clouds all day. It was early June and everything was deep green—thick forests we couldn't even see through, expansive velvet lawns, rows of corn flowing up and over the ridges. There were few people out and about, not even on the farms. Heading northeast in the foothills along the space between the coastal plain and the Appalachians, we constantly gained and lost elevation. It wasn't easy to see where we were going because the trees were so thick except when we were at the top with a view.

At the thirty-five-mile mark, we found Meadow Farm B&B in the middle of nowhere. It was delicious to soak in a hot bath and lie in a soft bed instead of squeezing into our small tent. The farmhouse dated from the eighteenth century with huge, creaky plank floors, low, plastered ceilings, old furniture and fixtures, and colonial prints on the walls.

We woke to heavy rain, the remnants of a tropical storm. The back roads were steep, like Ireland, poorly maintained with little or no shoulders, and curvy. Not ideal. We'd spend thirty minutes climbing a slope, five coasting down the other side—repeat. The traffic came up fast and close, scaring us. We pulled into the charming, wooded town of Wolfeboro and chose a quaint, white clapboard hotel nestled on the lake.

The inn was lovely but served a Woody Allen breakfast; lousy food and small portions. The sun came out and we were alternately entertained and intimidated by thunderstorms all afternoon. Trying to avoid traffic put us on rough, steep back roads. On one stretch, we climbed 1,200 feet in six miles only to discover the road was closed due to a washout from the storm. I was on the verge of a meltdown, so Jim approached the two-person road crew and asked if we could walk our bikes around their equipment and portage our bikes over the washout. And they said yes.

The other side of the washout was lovely, no traffic for miles through bucolic countryside. A sandy beach on Province Lake induced us to stop for a dip, and the bushes were close and high enough we opted to skinny dip. Back on the road, we saw a group of cyclists eating at a summer sandwich shack, so we stopped too.

"What's the best route to head into Maine?" I asked as we got in line behind them.

"Go north to East Madison, take 117 a few miles later. It's a little used back road, you'll feel like you're in Europe, going through towns with names like Denmark, Norway, Paris." After a yet another meal of burgers and fries, we followed the cyclists' advice, rolling up and down through the quiet forest. Several hours later, we slowed down to check out a gorgeous lakefront hotel, three-story white clapboard with banks of windows glistening in the sunlight. The road ahead could wait. We called it a day and booked a room with a view on the third-floor. Ten minutes after checking into our room, yet another drenching thundercloud passed overhead. It felt great to nail the timing, be inside and dry, looking out our big picture window as the storm pummeled the roiling lake. Even better, there was an indoor pool and a restaurant. After a swim, we went for dinner and found dozens of firefighters at the buffet. They were having their annual banquet after a day of fishing and were in a festive mood. One of the younger ones stopped by our table and started a conversation.

"I saw you two pull up on your bikes today. Your frames looked like they have some sort of odd joint." I watched Jim perk up at the mention of the couplings. Normally, he'd ignore a Mosquito, letting me answer, or walk away. Or both. But this guy asked about equipment.

"Oh, yeah," Jim replied. "We had our bikes machined, S and S couplings in Sacramento, our frames unscrew down for flying . . ." I took out my sketch book then, happy to capture the room while Jim chatted with the stranger.

"You should head to Farmington," the firefighter said, and at that I paid attention. "The college rents out dorm rooms in the summer. It's a nice town, too."

Thanks to the recommendation, we put in two fifties the next two days, following the cyclists' back roads into Maine, heading to the college town. Geography is destiny; on the East Coast, one either goes against the folds of the Appalachian mountains and pays heavily, or follows the folds on the ridges or valleys with less of a struggle. Thanks to local knowledge, we spent two days working with the hills.

As we slowed in the town of Norway looking for a place to spend the night, we encountered two young Quebecois men on lightly loaded bikes traveling from Montreal to Portland and back. They were surprised when we spoke in French. We were shocked to learn they averaged almost double our daily distance. They, however, were in their twenties, younger even than our kids—but still. They told us there are lots of great cycling routes in French Canada—planting a seed for our next trip?

We left town next morning with no breakfast because nothing looked appealing. In Buckfield, twelve miles later, Jim yelled "Look," and pointed to a hole-in-the-wall pizza/sub/breakfast shop, noisy and packed. Lesson #27: Follow the Crowds to Good Food. A restaurant parking lot filled with cars means better food, and, for me—because I love to people watch—better entertainment. We had eggs and homemade muffins based on the recommendation of the police chief at the next table, and the waitress kept our mugs filled with hot coffee.

Later that afternoon, we settled ourselves on the fifth floor of the brand-new Block Hall dormitory on the University of Maine/Farmington campus, high enough above the trees to provide a view of the town. Later, looking for a place to eat, Jim pulled me into a jewelry store and insisted I pick out something. I chose a lovely necklace of pink and green Maine tourmaline. After dinner, we followed the noise to a baseball game and found seats in the bleachers, until the "small-m" mosquitoes were eating us alive and drove us inside. What is it about mosquitoes? I feel like they have radar for fresh blood, my blood. They don't chew Jim up as bad; he's tortured more by the Mosquitoes.

On our last night before Bar Harbor, we got a room at a lovely farm B&B, Blue Hill, with rambling old buildings and a gorgeous yard. Lilacs bloomed everywhere, almost like weeds. Some white and some a very deep, deep purple. My mother had a huge lilac in the back yard, the scent sometimes made its way in my bedroom window. Lilacs always bring memories of May Day.

Much like in Hawaii, the lush green vegetation placed a real burden on maintaining properties. We saw scores of farmhouses on the back roads, many on the losing side of maintenance, especially the ancient ones. Some appeared abandoned and even the lived-in ones revealed few farmers out and about. Many of the occupied homes had signs out front, running small businesses out of their homes; small commercial as well as industrial and even creative industries—cabinetry, framing, pottery, fine-art painting. Some houses had the beginnings of gardens, most without fences (surprising, considering the deer), in rich brown soil. We didn't see many people out, even on sunny days. It wasn't as sparse as Idaho, but almost. The largest number of people we saw was at the ball game in Farmington and a Sunday afternoon high school graduation in Blue Hill.

The Bar Harbor Motel was a tidy, family-run motel with a colorful, hand-painted relief sign to help it stand out among the many motels on the road into town. We converged on June 11 for a four-day party. Jeanne flew into Albany from Hawaii, and my brother Eddie drove her with my father, Art, and Mother's widowed sister, Betty, in his big SUV. My father and brother were very familiar with the coast of Maine, while Jeanne, Betty, and Jim, and I had some catching up to do. Each day, Jim and I hopped on our unloaded bikes for at least a couple hours of riding, while Eddie drove the others, enjoying the splendor of Mount Desert Island with its many quaint roads, bucolic bike lanes, woods, and great views of the Atlantic.

* * *

By far, our favorite part of the day was finding a new place to eat lobster. Although once Eddie led us all to Thurston's Shack on the southwest corner of the island, we went back every day—it was that kind of place. As we entered Bernard, many lawns were piled high with lobster traps. Anchored boats, back from their early morning hauls, bobbed in tiny Bass Harbor. Thurston's stood out—bright yellow canvas roofs covered the two-story shack that hung out over the water. We impatiently waited in line to place our orders, then joined the diners at green wood tables and white plastic chairs; an ambience easy to maintain that can withstand the North Atlantic. Even though the sun was out and it was June, the space heaters were on and sheer plastic sheets were down to protect us from the wind and the cold. We dipped lobsters and clams served up in red and white paper bowls in clarified butter, washing it down with white wine in plastic cups.

Jim and my dad focused on the food, they both loved eating out—the finer the food, the happier they were. My mom's many years in a nursing home left my dad wistful; he loved to talk about old haunts and memories. Betty, an always impeccably dressed and coiffed widow, was the opposite, preferring to stay in the present and avoid the inevitable melancholy that followed. Eddie was great for that,

Chapter 23

joking with staff, customers, and was game to chat up anyone who came within earshot, to find out where they were from, what made them tick.

Arthur wore the same thick, moss-green fisherman's sweater every day, complemented with the red cotton golf hat he started wearing years ago when my mom's memory started fading—making it easier for her to find him in stores and parking lots. Arthur was why we were here the previous year for the first time since he reluctantly put my mom in a nursing home in June 1999. We got him to take a trip, four nights at Old Orchard Beach. That trip went so well we cajoled him into a repeat with my aunt. We all agreed on Bar Harbor, and Jim and I tacked on a week of biking beforehand.

Time to go, Jim and Ed tied our bikes down on his roof and we squeezed in the far back seat for the ride to Albany. We headed out to visit my mom before Jim and I flew home after our thirty-first bike tour since the Dordogne in '97, and our last before we'd retire and embrace a whole new kind of cycle touring—long-distance and long-term.

Stopping for a dip in Halfmoon Lake

New England forest

Riding unloaded on Bar Harbor Island

Beautiful Acadia National Park

TWENTY-FOUR

Game Changers

The Tuesday after Labor Day 2007, Jim came home from the Richmond refinery and announced: "That's it, I'm done." He took a breath and said, "It's time. I've been crunching the numbers for a while, and we can manage it." I'm pretty sassy, but after so many years together, I can tell when Jim's tone means I should just listen, so I did. He told me how fed up he was with work. We both had high-pressure jobs when I was first pregnant, only after the baby arrived we realized it was untenable. We both agreed I would switch to free-lance work from home. For thirty years Jim shouldered constant pressure while I happily flitted from babies to free-lance work to a return to school to part-time academia. The year before, Jim got a new boss who treated him poorly. He'd watched it happen to others before him. Forcing out high-salary older engineers to make way for newbies was a well-known cost-cutting strategy in the industry.

So he went into work the next day and gave notice. They were shocked—shocked enough to plead for time to find a replacement. In his many years at the refinery, managing the wetlands had become his bailiwick. They recognized he knew a lot of stuff no one else did; they needed time to find someone else and time for Jim to share his knowledge. He'd started on February 1, so it was decided he would go out on the same date. Five months seemed a long time. He would have left that day, but he agreed to stick it out.

Furthermore, I had already committed to teaching spring semester, and I needed time to process. Jim was ending a thirty-year career, but I had been an academic for less than ten. I was still an adjunct, my schedule at the whim of several East Bay campuses, from semester to semester. Maybe I could continue teaching for a few more years and Jim could paint, putter in the garden, do house repairs. I thought about this—ha!—for about two seconds.

Jim had another bomb to drop. "And I want to travel, now, or at least as soon as I quit working." He sprang it on me as we got up from the dinner table. "Let's just take off, *vamanos*, on the bikes. Let's be two nomads, rolling down a road with no end. Just keep going, see how long, how far, we can go." I did a sideways double take as I turned, looking for clues as to where this was coming from.

"Are you serious?" I asked in a quieter voice than usual. We had been talking about this for a few years now, since New Zealand at least. It'd been ten years since the Dordogne tour. The extent of some of our bike trips lengthened with the years, but most were ten days or less; only four trips were longer than two weeks, mostly because of the pressure from Jim's work not to be gone long. Jim wanted to take off and keep going. He was proposing a start date and no end date. I recognized the pattern, going all the way back to our first adventure in Yosemite, Jim proposed the ideas, my initial reaction was fear, then I got on board, joined in the prep and off we went.

But I wasn't there yet. I had many reservations. First, I liked my job and wasn't sure I wanted to walk away from all the work I'd put in. Then there were the kids. They'd both finished college, yeah, and that was a huge financial noose off our necks. But they were in their young adult years—

figuring out relationships, carving out careers, bouncing around different housing options. Their teenage aversion to hanging with their parents had diminished and we represented some solidity and certainty they could return to when they got banged up in the Real World. Unlike most of my friends from young adulthood, I knew early on that I wanted to be a mother. I loved being a mother, it was a primary part of my identity, and I wanted to be there for my kids.

I looked back most fondly on the first five years with my babies in our tiny house on Canyon Way. We were so poor, struggling to pay a mortgage that was more than three times the cost of the rental we left behind in San Francisco. Life was simpler, my babies so sweet and easy to manage before they went to school and life got complicated. How could I leave them just as they were fledging to adulthood? Even if they wouldn't say it, I knew they needed me. And I still needed them, and I loved being needed. Both were in relationships that might be taken to the next level. I couldn't be biking across Europe when they might need my help planning a wedding.

Plus, I loved teaching. Just walk away, *now*? And what about my online Western Civ class, all that work I put into it? On the other hand, we had come so far since the Dordogne Trip that Changed Everything, ten years prior. What had we learned? One thing we knew for sure was we both really did much prefer an open itinerary. And our strengths mostly complimented each other; Jim was the equipment guy, I was the mapper and the planner. Jim was the idea guy with me resisting at first but then jumping in and planning out the logistics. By now, you know this.

We learned a lot in those ten years. For Jim, the importance of top-rate, proper equipment. For me, maps with enough detail to make informed choices. This is harder than it sounds. Maps with a low scale that show the details of the back roads we preferred, well they take up a lot of space and weigh a lot. Get too large a scale with no back roads and they were worthless; too small a scale and the stacks of maps fill an entire pannier. Plus, the way we liked to travel, setting out with only a vague idea where we were headed, we sometimes found ourselves with no map.

The Garmin eTrex Vista HCx Jim bought in 2004 partly was another game changer. (Remember, these trips were all before smart phones.) I loved recording and analyzing our trip data. Paper maps rarely included elevation change data. At the end of a ride the Garmin was rich with info far beyond miles - riding time, resting time, climbing time. It had its limits, however, proving better for reaffirming data after a trip than helping plan one - our 2005 trip to Arizona, for example, The storms were unusual but we could have predicted the cold, the Garmin revealed after that we spent most of the week above 5000 feet. No wonder we were so cold.

Harbin Hot Springs also was a game changer—we fell in love with the place and almost all it represented. The spiritual aspect did nothing for us, but we respected the importance it holds for the current stewards. And Harbin was just the tip of the iceberg. It piqued our interest in all hot springs, anywhere and everywhere—the combo of cycling and soaking is magical. We brake for hot springs!

Tents were another game changer. Our first one lasted one night at Frank Raines campground in Stanislaus County. We could barely sit up in it, it was more of a two-person sleeve than a tent. If we were going to sleep in a tent and stay inside it for sometimes up to twelve hours, it had to be big and roomy enough for us to stretch and move about without being too heavy to carry. The second tent was bigger, but I loathed struggling to get ourselves and our gear in and out one door. "I want a tent with two doors" I had told Jim after only our second trip, to Harbin. "You can enter on one end, you and all your stuff, and I'll have the other end." We each managed our stuff differently. Two doors made the setups and breakdowns much easier. We went that weekend and picked out a two-door tent. Oh, I loved it. My own vestibule, my own pockets, my own space, me and my girls on one end, Jim and his boys on the other.

***

I felt myself coming around to Jim's way of thinking. His enthusiasm was contagious. But I realized I had my own agenda, too. I went into my office and came back with a map of the US, unfolding it on the dining room table. Way back in February 1970, I had posted a classified ad in my high school newspaper, *The Crossroads Gem*, looking for someone to cycle across the USA with me. That dream had never been realized. If Jim was serious about taking off then dammit, thirty-eight years later, we would do it together, west to east. But first, I had a few other things to get off my chest.

"I'm not quitting teaching before next May," I told Jim. "I already signed on for spring."

"Okay," Jim replied. "But, listen Anne, I want to travel, on our bikes. Like New Zealand but just take off. We're not getting any younger. If we really want to do this, it's best if we do it sooner rather than later. It'll be way easier to do now than in another ten years. What's more important—teaching or traveling?"

"It's not just teaching," I countered. "It's the kids, too. Quitting teaching is the easier part; I'm not tenured. But abandon the kids—just like that—for months, years? Is that what you propose? I can't do years, I just can't. Months, maybe, months I can try. And only until I become a grandmother."

Jim was listening. I kept going.

"If we do this, the first thing I want to do is bike from here to the East Coast." I reminded him of my teenage dream.

"How about come May we bike to Albany, or better yet, Bar Harbor? The family vacation last June was a blast, it'd be a great place to celebrate, and eat more lobster!" I was a little nervous if he thought I was raining on his parade. "Then we could come back home and check on the kids, the house, all that stuff, for a while. And then we take off again, in another direction?"

We looked at each other. We'd come so far together. I could see the excitement in his eyes, and I felt it rising up in me, too.

"Deal!" he said.

"Let's do it!" I agreed.

POSTSCRIPT

Looking back, I marvel at what Jim and I did, the places we went, the things we saw, the people we met. For ten years, we were Part-Time Nomads exploring much of our vast state of California, venturing further as we gained confidence. We bonded even more, sharing the experience of getting to know this wondrous world. I feel in my bones that I am a very different person today than I was when we cycled the Dordogne in '97.

For sure, we didn't realize what we were doing when we were doing it. One thing just led to another, our joining the tribe (and it is a tribe, just check out the website crazyguyonabike.com) wasn't planned. We thought our choices were pretty logical and reasonable, although we learned many of our nearest and dearest thought we were nuts.

On the morning of May 23, 2008, we biked down our driveway in Martinez and headed east, cycling along the Carquinez Strait, to the Sierras, the Rockies, all the rest in the middle, to the East Coast, all the way to Bar Harbor, Maine. For the first time we were moving together on our bikes completely free and unfettered, satisfied what we had learned, confident in ourselves and as a team that we could handle what came next.

After an "ah-ha!" moment, I started this book in June 2020 and quickly realized it wasn't a bad way to spend the Covid lockdown. I hadn't looked at the journals and photos of those ten years of part-time cycling since they were completed. Writing this book became a form of lockdown traveling, rediscovering our adventures while pouring over the journals, brochures, photos, and maps. I was surprised how much I'd forgotten, thrilled to revisit our adventures. I hope you've enjoyed coming along for the ride. And I've got lots more stories to share, give me time to get them down, pen to paper.

LESSONS LEARNED ON THE ROAD

#1: Pick your poison. Which fork in the road leads to the worst ride?

#2: Elevation, elevation, elevation! A mile climbing takes a lot more outa you than a flat road.

#3: Where's the food? Back roads are fun but often lacking amenities, follow them with a loaded larder.

#4: It ain't over until it's over. Close doesn't count, ya gotta get to the day's finish line before you let your guard down.

#5: Remember the world is a wondrous place. Seeing the world up close and slow on a bike only magnifies how beautiful this planet is.

#6: Following the water is dreamy. Flowing water adds eye candy and magic to a road.

#7: Travel cyclists attract Mosquitoes. Everyone you pass is going to want to know what the hell we are doing, and why.

#8: Geography is destiny. The landscape, topography, roads, and elevation can make or break a cyclist.

#9: Which is worse? A variation on Pick Your Poison, concerning choices other than forks in the road.

#10: The smaller the store, the crummier the food. In the US at least, more and more small stores are just purveyors of empty-calorie junk food.

#11: The best parts of a day's ride last the least amount of time. Savor the 5-minute descent after a 2-hour climb.

#12: To be a town, ya gotta have our Big Three. We can be pretty independent but a good grocery, better yet, also a good restaurant, and a library with wifi, are what we long for after a day on the open road.

#13: Bad things can happen to good food in panniers. Perishable food can get crushed and/or cooked in a pannier in a mere few hours on a hot day.

#14: All campgrounds are not alike. Less is more. What cyclists desire most at the end of a day - a shower, rest, a meal, are often not easy to acquire at campgrounds focused on motor vehicles.

#15: Cycling unloaded is heavenly. After days of cycling with gear that adds 25 to 50 pounds, riding without it feels feather light.

#16: Traveling by bicycle cancels campfires. Too cumbersome to carry wood, expensive in a campground, and too dangerous when free camping.

#17: If it's really hot and there's cold water, jump in. Better than a cup of coffee on a hot day, and back on the bike the wet clothes takes a while to dry.

#18: When one catches a downie in the mountains, enjoy it 'cuz you're going back up again. Never assume there are no more uppies down the road, until you stop for the day.

#19: We brake for cold drinks. Beer, lemonade, and water with ice are catnip to cyclists.

#20: Try it; If it turns out to be too hard, turn around. One doesn't really know if a route is impossible until you get there. And if it is, so what, just turn around.

#21: Things that seem scary at a distance aren't so bad up close. The worries of the night before usually melt away once you're in the thick of things.

#22: We make a pretty good team. It's just the bestest to have a True Bud to shoulder the hard parts together and celebrate the great parts.

#23: Beware of a "Gateway To" sign at the entrance of a town. The word "gateway" on a billboard or road sign means you are NOT to the main attraction, yet.

#24: Never assume. There's a vulnerability to road cycling that requires one to stay open and aware always.

#25: Preparation, preparation, preparation! Sure, it's great to know what you're getting yourself into, but spontaneity on a bike is also healthy.

#26: Quality equipment matters. Don't be penny wise but pound foolish with equipment.

#27: Follow the crowds to good food. A restaurant with lots of cars in the parking lot is a good barometer of a nice meal.

ABOUT THE AUTHOR

Anne M. Breedlove is the sixth of ten children born and raised in Albany, New York. Visiting San Francisco during a cross-country road trip in 1972, she decided to stay. After retiring from academia in 2008 she spent eight years traveling the world with her husband by loaded bicycle. She now happily juggles her time between art, bicycling, all things French, gardening, grandchildren, hot yoga, lap-swimming, printmaking, sewing, walking, and writing, but not necessarily in that order. Find me on IG: speedyab6 and on my website: annembreedlove.com

ABOOKS

Font used: Palatino Linotype, an OpenType version of the
Palatino font designed by Hermann Zapf in 1948
Printed on 50 lb. cream stock paper

ALIVE Book Publishing and ALIVE Publishing Group
are imprints of Advanced Publishing LLC,
3200 A Danville Blvd., Suite 204, Alamo, California 94507

Telephone: 925.837.7303
alivebookpublishing.com

www.ingramcontent.com/pod-product-compliance
Lightning Source LLC
Chambersburg PA
CBHW042041240426
43667CB00047B/2940